THE DOWN AND DIRTY GUIDE TO CAMPING WITH KIDS

The Down and Dirty Guide to

CAMPING WITH KIDS

HOW TO PLAN MEMORABLE FAMILY ADVENTURES & CONNECT KIDS TO NATURE

Helen Olsson

Illustrations by Scotty Reifsnyder

ROOST BOOKS | BOSTON & LONDON | 2012

Roost Books
An imprint of Shambhala Publications, Inc.
Horticultural Hall
300 Massachusetts Avenue
Boston, Massachusetts 02115
www.roostbooks.com

9 8 7 6 5 4 3 2 1

First Edition
Printed in the United States of America

⊗This edition is printed on acid-free paper that meets the American National Standards Institute z39.48 Standard.
♻This book is printed on 30% postconsumer recycled paper. For more information please visit www.shambhala.com.

Distributed in the United States by Random House, Inc.,
and in Canada by Random House of Canada Ltd

Designed by Daniel Urban-Brown

Library of Congress Cataloging-in-Publication Data

Olsson, Helen.
The down and dirty guide to camping with kids: how to plan memorable family adventures and connect kids to nature / Helen Olsson.
p.   cm.
Includes bibliographical references and index.
ISBN 978-1-59030-955-1 (pbk.)
1. Camping. 2. Outdoor recreation for children. 3. Family recreation. 4. Children and the environment. I. Title.
GV191.7.O57 2012
796.54—dc23

2011035883

To Quinn, Aidan, and Anya.

Campfire flames burn down to coals—
Ducks toast marshmallows on their poles!
Outside crispy, inside sticky,
Chewy, gooey, finger-licky.

—*Duck Tents* by Lynne Berry

CONTENTS

ACKNOWLEDGMENTS

First I'd like to thank my darling children for changing my definition of camping. While I miss the hours of quiet contemplation once associated with my camping trips, I relish the new moments of excitement, enthusiasm, adventure, and downright hilarity. They have given me a chance to see, once again, the natural world through the lens of a child. Simply put, there is little else that warms my cockles like the whoops and grins of my kids in the woods.

Thanks to my husband, Jeff, for his long-suffering patience, support, and for picking up the household slack at deadline times. Especially for his savvy IT support when evil digital gremlins corrupted my nearly complete manuscript at the eleventh hour. Without him I couldn't have completed the monumental task of writing a book about camping with kids, all the while mothering a brood of kids who camp.

Jeff and the kids, not to mention a few neighbors cornered next to the mailbox, served as guinea pigs for camp recipes. When I wasn't writing copy for the book, I was in the kitchen searching constantly for the perfect granola bar. I tried dozens of recipes and eventually made up my own. ("Okay, honey, this is batch eight: puffed wheat, not toasted, and rice syrup boiled for ten minutes instead of five. . . .")

Of course, if it hadn't been for my incredible parents, Mary and Gerry Burns, I would probably never have gone camping in the first place. They came to the United States from Northern Ireland in 1966, shortly after I was

ACKNOWLEDGMENTS

born. When I was a baby, they took a 26-day, 8,000-mile cross-country road trip, camping in the Great Smoky Mountains, the Grand Canyon, Yellowstone National Park, and in the desert outside Las Vegas. They saw America in a white Ford Fairlane with cherry-colored upholstery. In the backseat, my older brother and sister snuggled on a mattress in a nest of blankets and pillows. Which is to say: *they left me behind.* Left me in Buffalo, New York, with a friend of my uncle. Not even a close friend or relation or anything. Maybe it was because of that initial desertion that I've developed such a love of camping. I'm probably still making up for the slight.

Once my parents moved to the United States for good in 1968, they did take me along, and there were plenty of camping trips throughout the remainder of my childhood. In addition to providing basic lifelong inspiration, my parents were also helpful with the book itself, from reading chapters to babysitting the kids while I worked.

Thanks to my brothers and sisters (Gerard, Cathy, Peter, Stephen, and Clare Burns) for reading pages and advising me, but mostly for being interesting people. They served as great fodder for humorous anecdotes throughout this book. A special shout-out goes to my sister-in-law, Tanya Burns, who found the time to read nearly the whole enchilada, despite having a job and three kids of her own.

My gratitude goes to Megan McFarland and Dan Tucker, my agents. Without their hard work, dedication, and courageous decision making, this book would never have made it to print. Also to Jennifer Urban-Brown, my editor at Shambhala / Roost Books, for her careful consideration and attention to detail in the editing process.

Many folks read parts of the book and gave me valuable insights and feedback. Thanks to Kenny Ballard, Alex Bulkacz, Chris Casebolt, Linda Cohen, Helen Devereux, Catie McDowell, Gail Ross, Mary Shackelton, Evelyn Spence, and Bevin Wallace. Thanks also to those who advised me about the book business: Cindy Hirschfeld, Dimity McDowell, Paul Prince, Leslie Rioux, Tracy Ross, Claire Walter, Dana White, and especially Michael Stern.

INTRODUCTION

Fingers of flame lick the darkness and embers float skyward, melting into the night. It is mesmerizing. My husband and I are hunkered around the campfire with our three small children, relaxing after a long day spent hiking in the woods and tossing rocks into a lake. Our bellies are full of grilled burgers and corn on the cob, baked in foil right on the coals. We stretch out and sip red wine from enamel coffee mugs, while the kids, whose cheeks are smeared with chocolate, munch on s'mores. The roasted marshmallow oozing from between the graham crackers is a testament to the bliss of this perfect camping moment. In the sage words of my six-year-old son: "This is *awesome!*"

Even if the children's enthusiasm is mostly about the melty concoction of high-fructose corn syrup, it is at times like these, looking at the warm glow reflected on their chubby little faces, I realize that camping is the stuff of memories. Recollections of games played on an Xbox or Wii or whatever digital device of the moment, not to mention myriad episodes of "Superman versus Lex Luthor," will evaporate in no time. These camping moments are the snapshots they'll conjure up in their mind's eye when they think fondly of their youth. In fact, I'm kind of counting on this: that they'll reminisce about camping and not about the times I wouldn't let them eat Oreos before breakfast.

Camping can have the transformative power to shape a child's future experience. I know it did for me. I grew up in a family of six kids. Our parents regularly stuffed us into the back of a red Ford station wagon with a hodgepodge of gear and food, and carted us into the wilds of New Jersey and upstate New York. We hiked in our jeans and slept in an enormous canvas tent that had the water-repelling capabilities of a kitchen sponge. (How my parents mobilized half a dozen little campers remains a mystery to me.) I learned to love digging in the dirt, the crunch of leaves under my hiking boots, the smell of pine, and burrowing into a sleeping bag to the sound of cicadas chirping.

I never became a park ranger or Secretary of the Interior or anything like that, but I did have a career in the outdoor industry (I was an editor at *Skiing* magazine for many years). I love to ski and snowshoe in winter, camp and hike in summer. A brisk walk up a rocky trail—even with a thirty-pound toddler strapped to my back—does serious good to my soul. It's what rejuvenates me. And if I hadn't learned to love dirt at a tender age, today I probably wouldn't have a vegetable garden and three compost heaps in the backyard— and a thousand red worms wriggling in a bin under my kitchen table.

Better yet, a weekend in the woods with my kids provides a getaway from piles of dirty laundry, the Sisyphean task of keeping the kitchen counters clear, and the teetering mound of paperwork on my desk. With the usual noise of life drowned out, camping with kids affords you the luxury to just *be* with your children. To marvel at a wildflower or stop on a trail, close your eyes, and listen to the wind in the trees.

At home, my morning cup of tea goes cold on a daily basis, neglected as I run around in a frenzied whirl of multitasking. I end up heating it in the microwave about three times before I just give up. In camp, there's no microwave to nuke your coffee or tea, which means you simply have to sit down and enjoy it. For me, this is momentous.

When my brothers and sisters and I get together now (we are in our forties), we often revisit those childhood camping trips. The retelling is invariably accompanied by great belly laughs. One summer, we camped at the

Delaware Water Gap and went white-water rafting. Calling it "white water" was a stretch, because the water was unseasonably low. Really, there were only a few riffles to negotiate.

As we floated lazily downstream, the raft kept getting hung up on rocks. We'd have to poke and shove with our oars to dislodge it. My brother Stephen, eleven at the time, barked paddling directions: "Pull right! Pull right! No! Your *other* right!" But with multiple sets of oars in the water, we continued to beach ourselves. Stephen grew increasingly more frustrated, until he finally threatened to abandon ship. We figured the threat was empty; we were in the middle of a broad river, for Pete's sake.

Sure enough, the next time we got stuck, he said, "That's it! I'm outta here!" He stepped off the raft and onto a rock, where he crossed his arms and huffed. For thirty years, we have been giving him grief over this monumental lack of patience.

In addition to the lifelong benefits of camping, there are immediate health benefits. (Do not tell this to the kids.) Even beyond the hiking and swimming you might do while on a trip, the act of camping itself can be somewhat rigorous. When you need a pot of water to boil pasta, you can't just flip a tap. You have to *pump* it. Then you have to carry the sloshing water back to the campground. When I go camping, I feel as if my body has been in a constant state of motion all day, and it feels great—in a way that sitting at my computer pecking at a keyboard for eight hours straight does not.

Don't get me wrong: my favorite part of camping is putting my feet up on the rocks around the fire pit, drinking a cold barley soda stuffed in a coozie. But to get to that point, I've likely done a considerable amount of running about. At the end of a camping day, when you crawl into your sleeping bag, you feel as if you've channeled your inner caveman. You gathered the kindling, you fetched the water, you grilled the wild boar! Okay, so maybe you grilled organic, grass-fed steaks from Whole Foods, but you get the idea.

Our nation's children would benefit from a dose of the caveman lifestyle. On average, eight- to eighteen-year-olds spend four hours a day watching TV.

According to a study published in 2010 in the *Journal of the American Medical Association*, 31.7 percent of kids aged two through nineteen are overweight or obese.[1] And the Centers for Disease Control and Prevention report that the incidence of obesity in children ages twelve to nineteen has risen from 5 percent to 18.1 percent—more than tripled—since the mid-seventies.[2] Obese children are at risk for high blood pressure, high cholesterol, and type 2 diabetes, all diseases that were once considered strictly adult territory.

Camping is the perfect opportunity to increase children's physical activity while limiting their screen time. It's a chance to escape all those devices that flash and beep and require a thumb dexterity that I will never possess. Seeing the children darting through the trees around our campground, playing some imaginative game with sticks and pinecones—space alien hide-and-seek!—is simply priceless. It's a healthy gift to little bodies.

On a recent trip, the kids were actually making mud pies (to go with the mud stew). At home, if I told the kids to turn off the TV and make mud pies in the backyard, they'd grunt and moan as if I'd just suggested they scrape the ossifying banana peels from the cup holders in the back of the van.

In the national best seller *Last Child in the Woods: Saving Our Children from Nature-Deficit Disorder*, Richard Louv argues that a lack of direct contact with nature is putting our nation's children in peril. "A growing body of evidence indicates that direct exposure to nature is essential for physical and emotional health," Louv says.[3] He points to research that links obesity, stress, decreased motor coordination, lack of creativity, and even ADHD (attention-deficit / hyperactivity disorder) with an absence of nature in a child's experience.

Think of family camping as "nature therapy." In Louv's words: "Nature—the sublime, the harsh, and the beautiful—offers something that the street or gated community or computer game cannot. Nature presents the young with something so much greater than they are; it offers an environment where they can easily contemplate infinity and eternity."[4]

Although these priceless moments don't come entirely free, camping is a supremely economical way to vacation. When times are tight—and they so often are—camping is the way to go. No matter where you live, you can pack up the car and head for a campground, often in less than an hour's drive. No airfare required. And frankly, I'd rather eat live bugs than get on a plane with small children. With campsite fees running around $15 a night, the whole family can bunk down for a week for less than the price of one night in a nice hotel. Instead of racking up restaurant tabs, you can live off a week's worth of groceries—and likely eat healthier.

It's true that gearing up for camping can be an expensive proposition, especially if you are a gadget wonk and prefer your outdoor toys sophisticated. Rest assured, however, that there are ways to amass the essential gear for family camping without taking out a second mortgage. Either way, once you have the basic complement of gear, a camping trip will cost you very little.

The downside—and admittedly, there is a downside to camping—is that camping requires considerably more planning and packing than jetting off to Mexico with a couple of bikinis and a sand bucket. In fact, I was once so frenzied while packing for a camping trip that I broke my pinkie toe. Really, I did. Snagged it right on the leg of a kitchen chair.

You have a lot to organize before you go camping: There are the tent, the camp stove, and the flashlights. There are the pots and pans, the sunscreen, and the baby wipes. Not to mention the favorite pink fuzzy pillow, the Spider-Man pajamas, and baby's security blanket.

And there's just no waiting until 4:30 P.M. to figure out a camp dinner. Wing it on the menu, and you're going to be up a creek without a skewer when it's dessert time and you spaced the graham crackers. And binoculars and fishing rods and a book on butterflies. . . . The list goes on.

But here's the good news. There's a lot of spiffy high-tech gear on the market that makes camping easier and more comfortable than a generation ago. Certainly, tents have come a long way, from heavy cotton monstrosities to lightweight geodesic domes with collapsible aerospace-grade aluminum poles. Even camp chairs are infinitely more comfy than they once were. Remember those bulky folding chairs, the ones with the plastic strips woven piecrust-style across a stiff metal frame? Today you can get a portable camp chair with a padded seat, adjustable backrest, footstool, dual cup holders, and a bottle opener attached. I kid you not.

In the end, family camping is totally doable. You just need a plan—and you're holding it in your hands right now. Inside this book, you'll learn to master the art of car camping with kids. You'll find sections on choosing a destination, packing gear, planning a menu, and how to keep little tykes safe and engaged. Much of this book is dedicated to kid-related activities, ranging from the basics of hiking to detailed instructions for creating art projects using elements in nature. Throughout you'll find clever tips that will make your first time out that much smoother.

My first and possibly most important nugget of advice is to use checklists. I have a long list of lists, and this book is filled with them. Whenever we didn't bother to methodically check items off our lists, we headed off on one adventure or another only to realize three hours down the road that we forgot something essential. ("You packed diapers, right?" "Um, no.") Look for packing checklists throughout the book and tailor them to suit your family's needs and interests. These lists are also grouped together at the back of this book to make packing even easier.

May you, dear reader, benefit by learning from the multitude of mistakes my husband, Jeff, and I have made over the years with our children, Quinn, Aidan, and Anya. And though we've so often muddled through, those weekends in the woods have filled our kids with wonder. They've come home from camping trips tired and dirty but also inspired, fulfilled, and a little more confident than before. Camping trips leave us all feeling more connected to nature and to one another.

May yours, too, be a family of happy campers.

PART ONE

GETTING STARTED

A-camping we will go,
with monster friends in tow—
Hi ho the scary-O,
we dare you to say no.
We'll gather round the pit.
We'll growl, snort, and spit.
Hi ho the scary-O,
now grab a log and sit.*

—*Sipping Spiders through a Straw:*
Campfire Songs for Monsters
by Kelly S. DiPucchio

* To the tune of "The Farmer in the Dell."

"Emma!" Lizzie cried out, bopping up and down in her chair. "Guess what, guess what? We're going cramping."

"Not cramping, camping!" Ira said.

"That's what I said!" Lizzie said.

—*Emma Dilemma and the Camping Nanny* by Patricia Hermes

During Mass on my wedding day, the priest (incidentally, a drinking buddy of mine) took a moment in his homily to make a crack about my over-zealous planning. Something about the invasion at Normandy necessitating less paperwork than the day's blessed nuptials. There were to-do lists and general assignments for the wedding party. There were schedules, divided into ten-minute increments, for bridesmaids, flower girls, groomsmen, and guests. In my defense, however, let the record show that the whole operation went off according to plan and without incident. (There was a small matter of tequila shots for the toast being served in pint glasses, but otherwise it was the perfect weekend.)

I'm not saying you can't go camping on the spur of the moment. And if you ever find yourself with a few blank spots on your planner, a sunny stretch in the forecast, and all members in your party fit and healthy, then I say, pack up and go. Viva spontaneity! But if you're limited to summer weekends, when popular campsites fill up, you'll want to think ahead and be tactical.

You'll need to consider when, where, who (to go with), and how long to go for each trip. Following are tips and advice for planning around the seasons, special events, and weather, as well as the pros and cons of different locations and traveling with other camping families.

WHEN TO GO: SEASONS, SPECIAL EVENTS, WEATHER

Back when we were DINKS (dual income, no kids), my husband and I went on a winter backpacking trip near Brainard Lake, Colorado. Swaddled in Gore-Tex and giant mittens, we hoisted heavy packs and trudged into a blinding snowstorm. The snow was so deep that even with snowshoes, Jeff, who is not a small man, was breaking through the snow and sinking to his belly button. There were three couples in our party, and we set up our trio of tents in a grove of trees beneath Mount Audubon. With Everest-like aspirations, we intended to summit the peak that day. But with the deep snow, the hike in had taken hours longer than planned.

Instead we stayed at our base camp, huddled in the largest of the three tents drinking Bushmills and eating oysters on water crackers. We were warmed by the collective body heat inside the tent and the belly-burning tingle of the whiskey.

When we retreated to our individual tents, the warm glow quickly faded. My friends Pam and Brian nearly set their tent on fire when their stove exploded. My brother Steve kept stepping in a mantrap created by one of Jeff's snowshoe holes. He cursed, we chuckled.

That night, with our wet (and soon to be frozen solid) mittens and socks hanging on a line over our heads and both of us chilled to the marrow, I asked Jeff, "It's kind of fun, isn't it?"

His response: "We are never *ever* going winter camping again." And we never have.

Best Seasons: Anything but Winter

So here's my recommendation: Camp in summer, late spring, or early fall. Go when it's warm and sunny, and the nights seasonable. Cold kids are unhappy kids, so the fairer the weather, the easier it will be to keep the troops content.

The downside to summer is that everyone camps in summer, so you've got crowds to contend with. Summertime can also be buggy. In Minnesota, folks say the state bird is the mosquito; in Maine, the blackflies can be fierce.

Depending on the elevation and latitude of your camping destination, late spring or early fall can be less buggy and still pretty mild. In fall, you can add leaf peeping to your itinerary: camp among golden aspens fluttering in the breeze, sugar maples bursting in brilliant orange, and sumacs resplendent in deep red. In spring, you can hike through fields of pink, purple, yellow, and blue wildflowers. Trees will be budding, birds will be singing. And spring is when most wildlife has its young. Animal babies have huge appeal with kids, which explains the seven hundred stuffies scattered all over my house.

Check the Calendar

Camping is certainly an activity in its own right. And if your raison d'être is to be immersed in nature, just go camping. But maybe what you really want to do on a certain weekend is listen to bluegrass music, fill up on ribs at a barbecue, or quaff Guinness at a Celtic festival. Why not camp? That way you can party by day and sleep under the stars by night. Camping can enhance a special-events weekend or simply serve as affordable lodging.

If you think you'll want to do a night hike around a lake—or if you have kids who are afraid of the pitch dark—you might plan to camp under a full moon. Alternatively, if stargazing is on your agenda, camp during the new moon or attend a stargazing party. For guaranteed wildlife viewing, time your trip around a bird or butterfly migration, or even elk-rutting season.

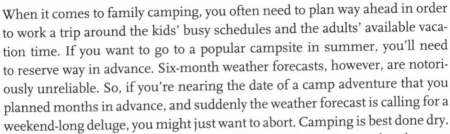

Meteorological Considerations: Weather or Not?

When it comes to family camping, you often need to plan way ahead in order to work a trip around the kids' busy schedules and the adults' available vacation time. If you want to go to a popular campsite in summer, you'll need to reserve way in advance. Six-month weather forecasts, however, are notoriously unreliable. So, if you're nearing the date of a camp adventure that you planned months in advance, and suddenly the weather forecast is calling for a weekend-long deluge, you might just want to abort. Camping is best done dry.

Of course, it's easier to pull the plug on a garden-variety weekend camping trip to a local haunt, because you can always reschedule. However, if you've booked the trip of a lifetime, say floating the Grand Canyon or flying by seaplane to a remote island, canceling may not be an option. If that's the case, just be sure to pack for the weather and then go for it.

On the other hand, good weather might inspire a trip. If a free weekend is coming up and the weather looks stellar, you might consider rallying for an unplanned trip and going to a first-come, first-served walk-in site. Bottom line: watch the weather.

Time of Departure: Morning Escape

In an ideal world, you'll set off on a camping trip early in the morning so you can set up the tent in daylight and have time for the kids to burn off energy and explore before dark. The alternative is leaving home in the late afternoon, driving right through the predinner witching hour, and arriving at a campsite with kids who are tired, hungry, and downright crabby in the pants. Pitching a tent in the dark is unpleasant enough even without kids, not to mention that tent stakes are infamous for disappearing after sundown.

Setting up camp under the cover of darkness is also not recommended for safety reasons. Two couples we know (who shall remain nameless in case anyone from Child Protective Services ever reads this) set up camp in the dark when their children were four years old. The kids played happily at the periphery of the campsite while the adults pitched the tent and unloaded the cars. The next morning, in the light of day, they discovered the kids had been frolicking just ten feet from a five-hundred-foot drop-off. Yipers.

Another benefit to arriving early, particularly in mountainous regions, is that you're less likely to get caught in an afternoon thunderstorm. If the tent isn't set up yet, you can't get into it and escape the downpour. Even in a drizzle, rain throws the proverbial wet blanket on the setup process. Try your best to get an early jump on your camping trip.

MOBCATION: THE MORE THE MERRIER

Camping is the perfect time to bond with your brood. When we've camped as a nuclear family, we've been able to bank lots of quality time with the kids. Those weekends feel low-key and intimate. But we've also spent many a camping weekend with other like-minded families. Sometimes called togethering, vacationing with extended family and friends can be a rewarding way to go. Before you commit to mob bonding, consider the pros and cons.

To be sure, camping with another family creates a different dynamic (read: raucous). Whenever you add more children to the recreation equation, you increase the chaos factor. It also means less one-on-one with your own little cherubs. When the kids' schedules are jam-packed with school, homework, sports, and playdates, you may relish those weekends in the woods with just you and yours. Having another couple along for the weekend also means diminished quality time with your mate. (Then again, if your spouse is in the doghouse, maybe that goes in the "pros" column.)

On the plus side, if you're new to family camping, you can learn tips and tricks from a more experienced family. And if you forget something, the other family probably has it. Having a collective gear pile on hand is a good thing when you run out of diapers or need a pair of tweezers to pull a thorn from a toddler's pudgy foot.

Kids love having friends to play with and, frankly, so do most adults. It's much more social. You can camp, commune with nature, and catch up on the neighborhood dirt. Camping with kith and kin can make mealtimes and the pre-trip food prep easier all around. Each family can be responsible for one night's dinner, and lunchtime can be a shared affair.

If you plan to share meals, a pre-trip planning meeting can be a lifesaver. Literally. If there are any food allergies in the group, all the cooks need to be onboard so you don't serve Pad Thai with crushed peanuts to a kid with a severe peanut allergy. Nothing ruins a camping trip faster than a case of anaphylactic shock. And I can tell you from firsthand experience, your Jewish vegetarian friends won't want you frying up your morning pork product in their camper. This is understandable.

Vacationing with another family also allows for sharing child-watching responsibilities. Adults can trade shifts as POD (Parent on Duty). One couple can take a short romantic walk or sneak away for a half-hour mountain-bike ride while the other couple runs herd on the rapscallions. The only time I've ever cracked a book on a camping trip (while the kids were still conscious) was when camping with another family. The dads took the wee people for a hike while the moms chilled at the campsite. It wasn't even Mother's Day.

If you're planning a trip with just one other family, you can make your reservations at the same time and secure side-by-side campsites. If you have more than two families, consider a group site, which can be more cost-efficient.

We once camped with a handful of families in a group campsite in southern Colorado. Our tents were so close that I could hear the dad in the next tent snoring (this falls in the "cons" column). The upside: I didn't have to sing to my babies that night. When he was putting his kids to sleep, he sang "Puff, the Magic Dragon." We just shut our eyes and listened. That, my friends, is synergy.

All campgrounds were not created equal. At one end of the spectrum are deluxe facilities with full amenities, such as showers, electrical hookups for RVs, and bags of ice for sale at a camp convenience store. At the other end are primitive campgrounds with walk-in, tent-only sites and Porta-Potties if you're lucky. The more primitive you go, the closer you get to the gestalt of backpacking.

Get a regional guidebook on your camping destination so you can read up on campgrounds. Online reservation systems also offer basic details and sometimes photos of campgrounds (see "Planning: Making Reservations" on page 13). One of the best ways, really, to find a great camping spot is to rely on recommendations from like-minded camping friends.

Location: Near or Far?

When it comes to selecting a destination, you need to consider this equation: the farther afield you venture, the less the crowds but the longer the drive. If you have little kids, the drive to the local library can seem eternal, so on your first few forays into the woods, it's best to stay relatively close to home.

Amenities: To Rough It or Not

When choosing a campground, consider how much you want to commune with nature (and by association, dirt). On the luxury side, modern campgrounds have bathing facilities, flushable toilets, water spigots, and sinks for washing dishes. Primitive campgrounds may have pit toilets and hand-pumped water, if that.

To me, pitching a tent in a primitive campground feels more like a genuine outdoor adventure. I like to brush my teeth and spit in the bushes with a view of the sun setting on a pristine lake. Primitive campsites offer a real immersion in nature. That said, my youngest has a very reasonable aversion to pit toilets, which causes us some undue distress around potty time when we're camping. You need to assess your crew's threshold for getting down and dirty.

Visitor Centers and Programs: Kid-Friendly Entertainment

If you choose to drive into a national forest and scope out your own solitary camping spot, you'll be entertained strictly by nature. This is a good thing. But with kids, sometimes you need extra diversions. National or state parks usually have visitor centers, which often have interpretive maps, hands-on educational displays, short films, and dioramas with stuffed bears, coyotes, and picas. They also have bathrooms, which always come in handy. Even smaller campgrounds may have nighttime presentations, educational talks, and guided walks. Be prepared to bail out if these programs are not designed for kids.

Urban Backstop: Lifeline to Civilization

Consider the proximity of a prospective campground to the nearest drug-store, phone, grocery store, and emergency room. My oldest son has severe food allergies, so we always like to know just how long it would take us to get to the ER. You might also want to know the drive time to the nearest grocery store in case you forgot something critical, like stone-ground mustard for the brats. (And I mean the kind you roast over the fire, not the ones in the backseat.) And because many campgrounds don't have cell service, you may need to scope out the closest landline for that conference call you couldn't worm out of.

Walk-in Sites: Lugging Distance

When making a reservation, take note of just how many feet it is from your parking spot to the tent pad. Some tent-only sites require a walk-in of as much as five hundred to a thousand feet. Even one hundred feet is consid-erable. Think of all the gear you have to get from car to campsite. Walk-in sites are usually lovely, because you get a dose of serenity that's not usually associated with car-camping sites. They are the perfect compromise between car camping and backpacking.

 If you're considering a walk-in campsite, call ahead to see if the campsites have bear boxes, which are large metal lockers for stowing food at night and whenever you're away from the campsite. Bear boxes greatly mitigate the lugging factor.

The trade-off is that you have to schlep your gear from car to campsite. And not just for setup and breakdown. For every meal, you'll need to haul the cooler down the path to your site. Once you've eaten, you'll need to haul it back to the car.

RV World: Camping in a Parking Lot

Once you've settled on a campground and you're booking a specific site online, make sure you're in the right neighborhood. If you have a tent, you don't want to be sandwiched between two massive recreational vehicles with portable AstroTurf lawns and satellite dishes out front.

Note to RV folks: at all costs, stick to the electric sites and avoid tent-friendly sites. You won't be able to plug in your camper, which means no microwave and no TV. Plus, you'll be surrounded by dirt-loving, tree-hugging tent campers roasting tofu pups over campfires.

Location Considerations

In the planning phase, you might choose a destination based on the type of activities available. If you have your heart set on canoeing, clearly you need to head somewhere with child-friendly waters and a respectable canoe outfitter nearby. For hiking with young children, look for campgrounds with short, mellow hiking trails nearby. And if your brood comprises fat-tire enthusiasts, pay close attention to the degree of difficulty of the surrounding trails. In mountainous regions, many mountain-biking trails are vertiginous, narrow, and strewn with rocks.

To give your camping experience an educational boost, check your children's school curriculum for the year. If they are studying the ancient Pueblos, perhaps you could camp near ruins of their cliff dwellings. You might seek out a campground near fossil beds to coordinate with a study unit on prehistoric life. Better to inspire a budding paleontologist with a visit to a national park to see the bones of a giant apatosaurus embedded in a cliff face than to plop your snuggle-bunnies in front of the big screen for another viewing of *Jurassic Park*.

Planning: Making Reservations

Before I had kids, I would happily drive into the night to some unknown destination and stumble around in the dark to find a campsite. (This is also how I once ended up pitching a tent in a gravel parking lot twenty feet from a busy road.) Once kids became a part of my camping experience, I was no longer willing to be so spontaneous. After several hours in the car, I need to know I have a place to stake my tent.

SMART TIP Find out ahead of time when reservations open for summer bookings. Put that date on your calendar. In big red letters.

That means advance planning. Popular campgrounds located relatively close to urban centers fill up quickly. Often you need to make reservations months in advance. Most campgrounds take reservations for campsites online or by phone. On the Reserve America website (www.reserveamerica .com), you can search by state, by park, by date, or by the kind of camping you want to do (tent, RV, or group).

When booking online, you can view maps of the campground. If you're camping with very small children, pick a site that's near the water pump and the restrooms (though maybe not right *next* to the restrooms). However, it's sometimes hard to pick the best site from a vague online map. If you plan to return to a campground after an initial trip, walk around the area with a campsite map and a pen. Mark the best sites, make a few notes ("shady and private" or "giant boulder for jumping off"), and keep the map as a reference for the next time you book online.

Not Planning: Playing the Unreserved Gamble

So maybe you're not so organized that you planned your summer trip back in May. But there's still hope: most campgrounds also have unreserved sites that are available on a first-come, first-served basis. If you go this route, call ahead and ask how early you need to arrive in order to get an unreserved site. In many cases, if you arrive by midmorning Friday, you can snag one of these sites. Arrive after dark, and you'll be looking for a hotel.

SMART TIP If you take a weeklong trip, you'll want to think about details like access to bathing facilities and a grocery store for restocking the camp pantry and refreshing the ice in the cooler. Then again, you can freshen up with baby wipes and survive on jerky and gorp for a good long time.

If your camping destination is nearby, one tactic for increasing your odds in the unreserved-campsite game is to send an advance crew to stake a claim. This works well if you're camping with another family. The stay-at-home parents and the kids can head for the campground early to secure the site, while the working parents can arrive later, after they've punched the clock.

HOW LONG TO GO: OVERNIGHT, WEEKEND TRIP, OR WEEKLONG ADVENTURE

You might be tempted to do an overnighter for your first camping trip. That's plenty of time in the woods for many people. A friend of mine will only camp on a one-night-stand basis, because she really needs to be in her own powder room to take care of business.

In my opinion, however, an overnight camping trip tips the scales of the effort-reward balance. After all the exertion of packing up gear, planning a menu, grocery shopping, and driving several hours to a campground, you ought to stay at least two nights.

Start out small with a weekend trip that's close to home. Once you've got

PREPPING THE KIDS

For some children, a first-ever camping trip can be a source of great anticipation; for others, a source of anxiety. It depends on the disposition of your child. The idea of sleeping in the woods in the dark can be scary for kids. If your child is the worrying type, there are steps you can take to help create positive excitement for an upcoming camping adventure.

1. *Start by reading books about camping and nature.* (See the resources section for book ideas.) Choose books that revel in the wonder of nature and all the fun of camping out. Avoid books about mountain lions snacking on small children. You might also pass over books filled with ghost stories. Telling scary stories around the campfire is a long-standing tradition of folklore. And to be sure, many kids love tales that raise goose bumps. But other kids are frightened by stories of headless horsemen and ax murderers on the lam. Go figure.

2. *Pull out maps and show kids where you'll be camping.* You can even go online and study hiking trails and campground maps to show them exactly where you'll be staying and exploring. Read about the flora and fauna found in the surrounding environment. Familiarity breeds confidence.

3. *Pitch a tent in the backyard.* Camping in your own backyard for a night can be a great way to test the waters. In fact, the National Wildlife Federation organizes a nationwide event every June called the Great American Backyard Campout. (For info, go to www.backyardcampout.com.) Grill up a camp dinner and eat it on a blanket on the grass. Then the whole family can crawl into the tent at bedtime—just feet from the back porch. It's camping without really cutting the cord.

A night in the backyard will help kids get used to the sounds of the night: the hoots of owls, the chirps of crickets, and the crackle of leaves as small critters shuffle through the underbrush. Explain to kids who are afraid of the dark in their own bedroom that camping out doesn't mean you have to sleep in the pitch black. During your backyard campout, let each child sleep with a flashlight under the pillow, and leave a portable night-light in one of the tent's mesh pockets.

4. *Encourage camping indoors.* My kids like to pretend to camp in their bedrooms, creating tent cities from pop-up play tents, blankets draped over chairs, and sleeping bags rolled out on the hardwood floor. They've even built fires in their bedrooms using Lincoln Logs for tinder and paper colored red for the flames. This is so much more responsible than the pretend camping my siblings and I did when we were little. Inside my brother's walk-in closet, we lit a real fire inside an old coffee can, which subsequently melted a perfect circle in the lime-green shag rug. This is not advisable.

the family camping experience dialed, explore farther afield and stay longer. Sometimes it takes two days just to decompress from the rigors of our everyday lives.

Once you've got the swing of things and you know your kids can hack it, go for a weeklong camping trip. This is the time to really unwind, enjoy the great outdoors, and bond with your kids.

Chapter Two

GEARING UP

G is for the Gear you'll need
To organize and pack
To keep your camping full of fun
And bring you safely back.

—*S Is for S'mores: A Camping Alphabet* by Helen Foster James

Once you've charted out a destination, it's time to gear up. But here's the thing about gear: the possibilities are ridiculously vast, and what you really need is relatively basic. On more than one occasion, I've had that classic parent-child discussion about the difference between "wants" and "needs." You *want* chocolate cake; you *need* your sleep. This is a critical semantic difference that's universally lost on kids. (And more than a few adults I know.) Camping gear breaks down along those same lines. You *need* tent poles; you *want* the twenty-piece grill set in the James Bond stainless-steel case.

Packing light is the backpacker's mantra. Every ounce counts, so the gear list needs to be pared down to the bare essentials. *Needs* only. But with car camping, you can add certain luxuries, like pillows and camp chairs. Even so, it helps to pack with an ultralight ethic in mind. Think travel-sized toothpaste and a mini-chessboard with magnetic pieces. Pip-squeak markers and stubby colored pencils. Matchbox cars and Polly Pocket dolls.

When you've got a minivan parked twenty feet from your campsite, it's easy to fall into the "jar of mayo" trap. Let me explain: My husband and I once rented a gear-toting sled for a winter hut trip. Despite the fact that we needed to use skis to physically haul every ounce we packed, not to mention a wriggly two-year-old in diapers, we overpacked simply because we could. We had the space, by George! We were tossing in hardback novels and six-packs of Guinness and full glass jars of Hellmann's mayonnaise. In the end, the sled swelled to an unwieldy 125-pound burrito that overturned every time the trail sloped a little. So even when you're car camping, it's better to pack a handful of your multivitamins in an old film canister and leave behind the industrial-sized container.

As you'll see on the following pages, even if you pack light, you'll pack a lot. We'll start with Hardware, a category that includes big-ticket items like tents and sleeping bags as well as the specialized list of camp gear required by kids, from portable potties to battery-operated ladybug night-lights. Next, find out how to gear up your camp kitchen in the Cookware section. The Softwear section will cover the essential wardrobe you'll need to stay cool in the heat, warm in the cold, dry in the wet, and screened from the sun. Finally, find shoes to keep your feet happy in the Footwear section.

HARDWARE: THE GEAR YOU NEED TO CREATE SHELTER

A cynical indoorsy friend of mine once said of camping, "Why would I want to pretend to be homeless for a weekend?" It gave me pause for a moment, until I visualized what our campsite looks like once we're settled in. A brightly colored high-tech tent filled with down sleeping bags and soft sleeping pads. A screen house draped over our picnic table. Comfy camp chairs tucked around a campfire. With the right pile of gear, we easily create a very comfortable home away from home. And if you think you're slumming it, just remember that in many nomadic tribes, even royalty lives in tents. Here's all the gear you need (and some you don't) to create cozy digs at the campsite.

The Tent

Arguably, the single most important piece of gear is the nylon roof over your head: the tent. With high-tech, water-repellent fabrics and collapsible poles, modern tents are light, weatherproof, and easy to assemble. The hardest part might just be choosing one.

Tents break down into two main categories: three season and four season. Three-season tents are designed for spring, summer, and fall. Four-season tents are built for camping in wet snow, freezing temperatures, and high winds. You can find inexpensive summer tents, but many of these are composed of mesh and a simple rainfly. (The rainfly is a separate piece of waterproof material that drapes over your tent. Some cover the roof only; others cover the entire tent.) If you're in a summer tent and the temperature dives at night, which often happens at higher elevations, you'll be shivering, and if a thunderstorm rolls in, you'll be sodden.

Another type of tent is the three- to four-season convertible variety. To adapt to different weather conditions, convertibles come with extra poles, add-on vestibules, and panels that zip off to expose mesh. Frankly, it sounds like more bits and pieces to lose in the black hole of your garage.

Which brings us back to those two main categories. Four-season tents (also called mountaineering tents) are built tough to keep you warm and dry in extreme conditions. Perfect if you're planning to ascend Ama Dablam. They tend to compromise on ventilation, which means that such tents can be stifling during the summer. And there's nothing worse than an overheated

SMART TIP Be aware that when manufacturers call a tent a "four-man" tent, they are assuming that bodies are being lined up inside, in alternating head-to-toe directions, like shrink-wrapped ballpark franks. If you want some breathing room for you and your brood, your gear, and maybe even the family dog, you might go with a six- or eight-man tent for a family of four.

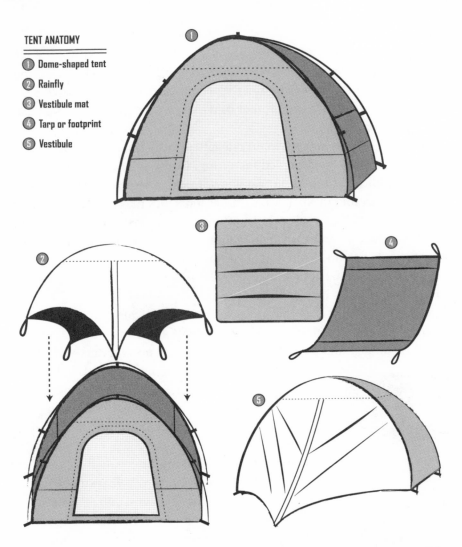

TENT ANATOMY

1. Dome-shaped tent
2. Rainfly
3. Vestibule mat
4. Tarp or footprint
5. Vestibule

toddler on a sweltering day. All that technology comes at a price, too: top-of-the-line, expedition-style two-man tents can run as much as $550. And a family, by definition, would need more than a two-man tent.

If you plan to camp only in the more seasonable months—and truly, only the hardiest of parents would drag their kids into the woods in the winter and camp in a tent, and I'm not one of them—you'll want to go with a three-season tent. Depending on a multitude of factors, a three-season family tent can range in price from $50 to $600. When it comes to tents, you really do get what you pay for. Remember, the tent is the very slim barrier between you and the elements, not to mention pterodactyl-sized mosquitoes. This is the time to splurge, people. The better tents, from companies like The North Face, Mountain Hardwear, and Marmot, are built to last.

For car camping, families will want a roomy, base-camp style—either a cabin shape or a dome shape. (Tents also come in A-frames, tubular shapes, and more.) We have one from Kelty that feels downright palatial: My six-foot-two-inch husband can nearly stand upright inside. When our youngest was a baby, we would set up a crib on one side and drape the tent's fabric wall down the middle. My husband and I actually had our own room.

Another thing to look for when you're shopping for a tent is a sturdy rain-fly. This is the gigantic canopy that drapes over the inner tent, suspended with poles and tied off with bungees and guylines. For all your mud-caked hiking boots and maybe even your bags, you'll want a tent with a roomy vestibule, which is created by the rainfly.

Look for a tent with waterproof (or at least water-resistant) wall materials, as well as a tub floor (meaning that the extra-durable flooring material of the tent extends several inches up the sidewalls, creating a tub effect). Check your tent's instruction manual to see if you need to waterproof the seams of your new tent before you first use it. Most quality tents come with seams sealed at the factory. You'll want a tent with lots of mesh pockets to stow glasses, water bottles, headlamps, and tiny Lego men. If you're camping in warm climates, look for a tent that has good ventilation.

When deciding on a tent, you'll need to run an algorithm of weight, space, durability, and cost. Manufacturers use high-tech fabric to shave weight from tents, so the lighter the tent, the higher the price. If you think someday you'll be backpacking with your kids, you might consider paying more for a lightweight tent. If you know that all you'll ever do is car camping, go ahead and get a heavy mansion of a tent where you can really stretch out and maintain your personal space bubble.

SMART TIP Before you plunk down your credit card, set up a prospective tent inside the store to see how easy it is to assemble. Then crawl inside and lie down to get a feel for how roomy it'll be with the whole family and your gear.

Play Tents

Consider bringing along a play tent or an old tent from the attic to let the kids play in during the day or while you're setting up camp. You can also find pop-up play tents at any toy store. They store flat with a deft fold and twist, so you can easily slide them between gear in the car. Get one with Thomas the Tank Engine or Disney fairies and a tunnel entrance, and you'll keep the kids out of your neat and tidy main tent.

The Tarp

Between the tent floor and the dirt, you need a tarp, a.k.a. ground cloth. It's an extra barrier between you and the wet ground, and it helps protect the underside of your tent from sharp rocks and other prickly bits. When it rains, the tarp becomes a critical element of your tent setup.

We've always gone the el cheapo route on the tarp, buying one of those big blue plastic tarps from the hardware store. Because our tarp is bigger than the tent floor, we end up doing a considerable amount of tarp origami to get it the right size, which is slightly smaller than the tent floor. See "Pitching the Tent" on page 66 for more on tarps.

Tent manufacturers like Big Agnes, REI, and Mountain Hardwear sell "footprints," lightweight nylon tarps shaped precisely to fit under specific tent-floor sizes. These usually run from about $20 to $60. Footprints have the added benefits of being lightweight and having elastic loops that hook onto your tent poles.

Sleeping Pads

"What's a dirt nap, mom?" my daughter, Anya, asked when she was four. I told her, in age-appropriate lingo, that a dirt nap is a euphemism used by the Mafia to describe being dead. She pressed on: "But what about camping? You're sleeping in the dirt, right?"

She had a point. But really, with today's sleeping pads, it's one very comfortable dirt nap. Car camping affords you the comfort of a truly good night's sleep.

In our backpacking days, we brought wafer-thin sleeping pads and the lightest possible sleeping bags. For pillows, we packed fleece shirts into the stuff sacks from our sleeping bags. The cricks in our necks in the morning proved we were roughing it. Now when we car camp, we make our shelter not unlike a royal Bedouin tent. Comfort is king.

There are four basic types of sleeping pads. First, there are closed-cell foam pads, like the ones we once took backpacking. They are constructed of a dense waterproof material that insulates well but compromises on comfort. "Firm" is the word that comes to mind.

Second, there are open-cell foam pads, which are softer and cushier, though not as good at keeping you toasty. For about $20, you can get a simple, inch-thick open-cell foam pad shaped like an egg carton. These pads offer surprising comfort and enough warmth for summer camping. The downside is bulk: they roll up to about the size of a redwood log.

The third option is an inflatable pad. For backpacking, you'll find manually inflatable pads that are high-tech, low weight, and pretty pricey. For car camping, a better bet would be a self-inflating sleeping pad, which is a cross between an inflatable pad and a foam pad. Starting around $65, there are all manner of self-inflating sleeping pads from companies like Therm-a-Rest, Big Agnes, and REI. These pads have closed-cell foam wrapped inside a water-resistant nylon outer layer. At the high end are three-inch thick, self-inflating mattresses with built-in foam pillows and soft microfiber covers, which run about $200. If you think you'll graduate quickly from car camping to back-packing, go for a lightweight (less than two pounds) inflatable pad that can pack down to the size of a loaf of bread.

A fourth option, albeit an unwieldy one, is to use one of those fully inflat-able, foot-high air beds. To inflate it, you'll need an electric pump that runs on batteries or that plugs into the car's cigarette lighter. We went the big air-mattress route once, but the kids ended up turning the tent into a gymnas-tics arena, and the mattress (read: trampoline) subsequently sprung a leak and deflated. We pretty much spent the night sleeping on the ground.

Most sleeping pads are twenty inches wide. If you think Junior will want to snuggle between you and your spouse, consider larger-sized pads, either twenty-five or twenty-nine inches wide. The extra width is a bonus if you roll around in your sleep. Or consider a pad designed to sleep two: Big Agnes has a fifty-inch, double-wide pad that can be paired with the company's double-wide sleeping bag.

 **SMART TIP** If you're camping when the ground is very cold or wet, purchase a few inexpensive closed-cell foam pads as an insurance policy. You can place the closed-cell foam pad, which is waterproof and a good insula-tor, underneath your comfy open-cell foam pad or inflated pad. You'll stay toasty, and if your inflated pad springs a leak, you've got a backup layer.

For kids, there are only a few child-specific sleeping pads on the market. For instance, Pacific Out-door Equipment offers a pint-sized pad complete with a Sharpie and a built-in growth chart. Your best bet is probably buying small-sized adult pads, either short or three-quarter-length, which are designed for reducing pack weight in the backcountry.

Sleeping Bags

Sleeping bags come in many shapes, sizes, and fabrics. The first thing to consider is whether you're going to upgrade from car camping to backpacking someday. We were shortsighted on our first sleeping-bag purchases and bought giant, heavy rectangular bags for car camping. They were roomy and comfy, and we didn't have to dip into the kids' college fund to buy them. Weight and bulk were a nonissue. But when the time came for our first backpacking trip with the kids, we realized we needed to buy all new bags. We needed compressible lightweight bags for the backcountry. Now we have so many sleeping bags our basement looks like a Campmor warehouse.

Sleeping bags are categorized by temperature. In theory, a -10 degree Fahrenheit bag would keep the average camper warm in -10 degree weather. For most summer camping, you'd need a bag rated only to 35 or 40 degrees Fahrenheit. Maybe even higher if you're camping in the desert.

Sleeping bags are generally filled with either down or synthetic fibers. Down is soft, light, long lasting, and can compress into a small package for travel. The downside to down is that it's pricey and doesn't dry quickly when wet. The latter can be problematic if you're camping in a soggy environment or if you have a bed wetter in your brood. Synthetic bags are sturdy, quick drying, affordable, and warm even when wet. But they can be bulky.

SMART TIP

Pack an extra sleeping bag in case of nighttime accidents. There's no such thing as changing the sheets at midnight when you're camping.

Car-camping bags tend to be rectangular in shape, which makes them spacious and comfortable, but hefty. The mummy shape of most backpacking bags cuts down on the amount of material used, which cuts down on weight. The mummy shape also creates less airspace inside the bag, which means you can warm up quickly.

For camping with a small clingy child, you might consider two adult bags that zip together so your little cupcake can squeeze in. My kids are savage kickers at night, so they get their own bags. Many companies offer child-specific bags, which are shorter and narrower than adult bags. The smaller the air pocket inside the bag, the easier it is for kids to get toasty. Our kids seem to have high-combustion internal furnaces, so they sleep fine and stay plenty warm in adult bags. If your child runs cold, consider a child-specific bag. They're cheaper, though kids will eventually grow out of them.

SMART TIP To keep active sleepers from rolling off the sleeping pad, look for a sleeping bag that has side loops and straps that wrap around the sleeping pad to keep the bag affixed to the pad. Other sleeping bags have built-in sleeves to keep the pad in place.

The Vestibule Mat

The rainfly on most family-sized tents creates a roomy vestibule just outside the tent's front door. This is a good place to store any bags that don't fit inside the tent. When you go exploring for the day, you can toss camp chairs inside the vestibule to keep them safe from wind and rain. The best part of a vestibule is that it creates a place to leave boots, sneakers, and sandals so you can keep the tent a shoe-free environment.

In front of the tent entrance, we usually set down a small tarp and use it as a giant welcome mat. The trouble is that after a day or so, there's a layer of dirt *on top* of the tarp, defeating its purpose to an extent. An ingenious solution to this problem is a sand-defying mat by a company called CGear. Developed as a landing pad to reduce dust and sand kicked up by the rotors of military helicopters, the CGear mat allows small particles like dirt, dust, and sand to fall through the rug but not migrate upward.

The Screen House

If it starts to rain buckets, you can always retreat to your tent. But if the weather arrives just as you're ringing the dinner bell, you've got trouble. One way to cover yourself is to buy a screen house that you can erect over your campsite's picnic table. When the weather is fair, you can roll up the walls and then drop them when the precipitation starts.

Companies like Kelty and REI make lightweight structures for this purpose. You can also create your own shelter with a tarp, collapsible tarp poles, and ropes tied off on rocks and trees. This is when those knot-tying skills will come in handy. See "Knot Tying," page 153.

See "Knot Tying," page 153.

HARDWARE CHECKLIST

- [ ] Tent (with poles, stakes, and rainfly)
- [ ] Tarp (ground cloth)
- [ ] Extra plastic tarp
- [ ] Rope
- [ ] Vestibule mat
- [ ] Sleeping bags
- [ ] Sleeping pads
- [ ] Pillows
- [ ] Screen house
- [ ] Play tent
- [ ] Camp chairs
- [ ] Lantern and mantles
- [ ] Flashlights or headlamps
- [ ] Spare batteries
- [ ] Day packs
- [ ] Small mallet (for pounding tent stakes)
- [ ] Ax

Camp Chairs

Camp chairs are one reason that car camping rocks. In the backcountry, you're lucky to find a knotty log or a bumpy rock to sit on—and let's face it, after a while that kind of seat is going to give you a sore butt. Our camp chairs are more comfortable than my kitchen chairs by a long shot. Look for collapsible fabric chairs with sturdy metal legs, cup holders, and maybe even a bottle opener attached.

If your mission is to be a camp potato, consider a recliner or chairs with built-in headrests and footrests. Portable, legless, foam backpacking chairs, the kind that lie on the ground but provide you with a cozy backrest, are great for around the campfire, too, as long as your knees are supple enough to stand back up again. Crazy Creek, Kelty, and REI make these chairs.

GEARING UP

Flashlights, Headlamps, and Lanterns

At night, camping is a little like a New York City blackout, but without the looting. It's dark. To be without lights means you can enjoy the glow of the fire and the sparkle of stars overhead. Still, sometimes you need to see what you're doing. Headlamps, little glowing orbs of light that strap to your cranium, are surely the handiest light source for campers. They allow hands-free illumination for washing dishes, zipping up little coats, or reading *Goodnight Moon* around the campfire.

There are a variety of lightweight, low-profile LED (light-emitting diode) headlamps on the market from companies like Petzl, Mammut, and Black Diamond. These days, most of the headlamps available have LED bulbs as opposed to incandescent. The first LED headlamps we used didn't seem nearly as bright as the old-school lamps, but the technology has caught up. LEDs use less battery power, last longer, and are more durable than traditional bulbs. Kid-specific headlamps feature brightly colored bands and lamps shaped like Lego men or zoo animals. There's one shaped like a frog. It even croaks when you turn it on.

SMART TIP Stash a headlamp or small flashlight in your pocket *before* the sun sets. Once it's dark out, you'll have trouble finding a flashlight in the bottom of a bag that's somewhere in the tent.

Flashlights work for camping, too, and you can get a level of beam power in a big flashlight that you won't get from the strongest of headlamps. Another advantage: when a fellow camper carrying a flashlight looks you in the eye, you don't get blinded in a way that violates the Geneva Conventions. Maybe you just like the security of a two-pound Maglite in your palm when you're walking to the bathroom in the pitch black. (You can't really whack a bear upside the head with a six-ounce headlamp, now can you?)

For backpacking, headlamps are a must. Most are the size of an egg and weigh less than an apple. But if you're car camping, a big lantern that you can set on the picnic table is handy, especially for cleaning up after dinner or setting up camp if you arrive after dark.

SMART TIP To avoid kerfuffles, issue one headlamp per child. Sharing is good, but when it comes to wielding a piece of gear that is not unlike a Star Wars light saber (or "light saver" as my kids call it), you can just forget it.

There are gas-powered lanterns and battery-powered lanterns. We've always used the traditional Coleman fuel-burning lantern—the green one with the wire handle and the glass globe encasing the little glowing white mesh baggies (called mantles). It throws a tremendous amount of light and reminds me of camping as a kid. But it's a bit noisy, it's another thing the kids can burn themselves on, and I break the glass globe about once a trip. Electric lanterns aren't as powerful a light source, but they are quiet, safe, and rugged. Whatever light source you choose, make sure you bring enough fuel or batteries.

If your child is used to sleeping with a night-light at home, add some cute battery-powered night-lights to your camp-gear arsenal. Or bring a half-dozen little glow sticks. Before bed, the kids can play with them (light show!). Then tuck the sticks into the tent's mesh pockets, where they'll give off a soft, comforting glow.

Day Packs

If you plan to hike while you're camping, remember to bring along a few adult day packs. Osprey, Gregory, Kelty, and The North Face all make well-designed, comfortable packs. Rather than a top-loading model, go for a pack that has a U-shaped zipper so you can easily zip off the front panel when you're rooting around for lip balm. Between the adult packs in your party, make sure you have enough room for the backcountry travel essentials (see

DUCT TAPE: WONDER FIXER

Duct tape, that silky, silvery miracle tape of infinite possibility, might be the single handiest multipurpose fix-it tool in your gear box. It is the ultimate mechanism of improvisation and resourcefulness. Just ask MacGyver. (Ironically, duct tape should never be used to seal ductwork.) My brother Peter once used duct tape to keep the swaddling blanket on his newborn from coming unraveled. This was before swaddling blankets came with Velcro, mind you.

We've used duct tape to repair a broken tent pole, pad blisters, and hold down the top of our cartop rocket box when it sheared off like a tuna-can lid on a windy day. Toss a roll in with your camp gear. If you're backpacking, roll a three-foot-long length of duct tape around a flat bit of cardboard. And if you think you don't need duct tape, consider this: when NASA's astronauts head for space, they always bring duct tape.

A DOZEN CAMPING USES FOR DUCT TAPE

1. Patch a hole in your tent, tarp, or rainfly
2. Temporarily repair a broken tent pole or zipper.
3. Cover a hot spot on the foot to stave off a blister.
4. Patch a hole in a glove, a sneaker, or a pack.
5. Cinch up a delaminating boot sole.
6. Patch a split up the back of your shorts.
7. Temporarily repair a crack in a canoe or kayak.
8. Use with a bit of gauze to bandage a wound.
9. Wrap a sprained ankle (over the sock, unless you also want to use duct tape for hair removal purposes).
10. Fashion a makeshift splint.
11. Immobilize an injured finger or toe by taping it to its neighbor.
12. Seal the frayed ends of ropes and shoelaces.

LITTLE TYKES GEAR
CHECKLIST

☐ Front-loading baby carrier
☐ Baby backpack carrier
☐ Portable crib
☐ Kid-sized day pack
☐ Child's reusable water bottle
☐ Portable potty or potty seat
☐ Portable high chair
☐ Child-sized folding camp chair
☐ Battery-powered night-light
☐ Child-sized or small adult
   sleeping pad
☐ Child-sized sleeping bag

page 215), which include food and water. A pack in the neighborhood of thirty liters should do it. Also see "Kid-Sized Day Packs" on page 33.

If you prefer to drink from a hydration system rather than from bottles, be sure to look for a pack that will accommodate a hydration reservoir. Although packs with mesh pockets and small zippered compartments are handy for organization, I recommend avoiding packs with too many compartments. We have one particular day pack that has so many zippered compartments, we can never find anything. We've lost half-eaten energy bars in that pack for months at a time.

LITTLE TYKES HARDWARE:
SPECIALIZED GEAR FOR SMALL CAMPERS

In many ways, family camping is not so different from couples' camping. Regardless, you need tent, sleeping bags, lanterns, and so on. With kids, you need all that gear and more. And when it comes to kid-specific gear, if you forget certain items, you're in deep doo-doo. (Literally, if it's diapers you forgot.) On more than one camping excursion, we forgot our child backpack carrier. On hikes, we ended up carrying our youngest in our arms, which is thoroughly exhausting, and on our shoulders, which is just downright dangerous on a rocky trail. It's also an easy way to clothesline your kid on low-hanging branches.

Baby Backpack Carrier

The best thing about camping with babies and small toddlers is that you can stuff them in a baby backpack carrier and truck on down the trail at your own pace. Most babies and kids will get rocked to sleep by your rhythmic hiking, so in the end everybody's happy. You got your hike; Junior got his nap.

For infants, there are soft, lightweight front carriers where your pumpkin can snuggle into your chest and you can be hands-free. Snugli and Baby Björn make front-loading infant carriers. Back-mounted child carriers function much like backpacks. They have external aluminum frames, adjustable shoulder and waist straps, and compression straps to keep the pack snug against your back. Child carriers often come with five-point harnesses; pint-sized, zip-off day packs; and compartments for diapers and changing pads. Look for a carrier that has a shade for rain and sun so you can protect little ones from the elements.

The most important thing is that the child carrier fits you and your torso properly. The better the fit, the more comfortable you'll be carrying the load. Most carriers will tote a child up to forty pounds. Once kids start pushing that envelope, it's essential to have another adult help hoist the pack. When I was pregnant with our third child, I went snowshoeing with my son Aidan, who was at least forty pounds at the time. When I first tried to get the pack on (by myself), we both tipped over backward. I ended up flat on my back—on top of Aidan—like an overturned turtle.

Kelty has neatly designed carriers with spring-loaded kickstands that deploy and retract automatically. Sherpani makes a really comfy ultralight carrier that weighs less than five pounds. And Deuter has a day pack that unzips to reveal a padded seat and harness.

Portable Crib

When my oldest son, Quinn, was a baby, we went backpacking in Steamboat, Colorado. Getting to sleep without the close comfort of his crib walls was beyond difficult for him. All snuggled up in the sleeping bag, he spent forever giggling at the *zit-zit* sound of his fingernails scratching against the wall. We thought he'd *never* get to sleep. After that, when we car camped with the kids, we would bring along a portable Pack 'n Play and set it up inside the tent. (This is where a monster-sized tent comes in handy.) When it was time for naps, time for bed, or just time for a time-out, we could plop them into the portable crib. At night, they slept well because the setting was so familiar. And when kids sleep well, so do their parents.

Kid-Sized Day Packs

It's a good policy to get kids to carry their own gear early on, even if all they have in their pint-sized pack is a stuffed bear and a water bottle. Plus, when children carry packs, they look like real campers. REI, Osprey, Deuter, The North Face, and Kelty make packs designed for a child's small torso and dainty hip circumference.

SMART TIP

To protect little spines, make sure your child's pack weighs no more than 20 percent of his or her body weight. Look for backs with good hip belts, which help distribute the pack's weight so it's not all hanging on their shoulders.

For day hikes, kids need only simple day packs, which can also serve as school backpacks for books and lunch. If you think you'll eventually head into the backcountry with your kids, look for child-specific backpacking packs, which are higher-tech, higher-priced, and designed to tote more. Some packs add clever features like safety whistles attached to the buckles. Others just add whimsy, with bright colors and fun kid prints, from birds and flowers to the contour lines of a topographic map.

Water Bottles and Hydration Systems

Each child should have a dedicated kid-sized reusable water bottle. Look for bottles in stainless steel or BPA-free plastic. Avoid bottles with screw-on caps. It's hard for little hands to screw tops on and off, and the tops will undoubtedly get lost. Go with pop-up straw tops, pull-up spouts, or even sippy-cup lids. Klean Kanteen and Nalgene make basic kid bottles; Sigg, REI, and CamelBak make them more fun with cute graphics, from pirates and T. rexes to fairies and butterflies.

CamelBak also makes backpacks with integrated hydration systems. The water is stored in a bladder inside the pack, and kids drink through a tube-and-nozzle system. Hydration systems are great because they allow for hands-free drinking, they are less likely to be left behind after a water break, and drinking from a tube is like drinking from a giant flexible crazy straw.

Kid Toilet: The Pint-Sized Porta-Potty

I've had camping trips where I swear I spent half the time in the campground's bathroom. This is unpleasant. My daughter didn't much like the pit toilet, so she wouldn't go . . . but she *had* to go. So we went a lot. On the next trip, even though she was old enough to use an adult toilet, we brought along the little potty we had used for toilet training. We set it in the vestibule of the tent so if she had to go (again), she could go right there. It saved us countless trips to the john. And at night, having the potty just outside the tent is mighty convenient.

Portable High Chair

For small toddlers and for babies who are sitting up and eating solids, a portable high chair at mealtimes can be a godsend. Most car-camping sites have picnic tables, so you can use the clamp-on variety of portable high chairs.

Most couples who are planning to camp with kids have camped in their life B.C. (before children), which means they probably have some gear collecting dust in the basement. But if you don't own a single tent stake, gearing up from scratch can be an expensive proposition. If you want to test the waters of family camping before fully investing in all the requisite gear, you might consider borrowing gear.

First, hit up friends who camp. They'll let you borrow their tent for free. (And their sleeping pads, and camp stove, and lantern. . . .) But remember how Barney never returned the rock lawn mower to Fred? No sense losing friends over a wayward compass.

For a fee, many outdoor stores will let you borrow gear. Big chain stores like REI and EMS rent tents, stoves, backpacks, sleeping bags, sleeping pads, and bear canisters. Try your local camping store; it might rent gear, too. These days there are also online companies that ship the rental gear to you. This is a good option if you are flying somewhere and want to camp while you're away. Having rental gear delivered to your destination will save you paying the airline for extra baggage. The website www.lowergear.com rents not only major gear items but also accessories, from headlamps to cooking pots to bear spray.

A gear-rental site called www.outdoorsgeek.com gives you a "Try it before you buy it" option. You try out (rent) the gear for a given trip. If you like the gear and want to keep it, the company applies your rental fee to the price of the equipment.

However, the tops of those picnic tables may be too thick for some hook-on chairs. Depending on the child, a portable booster seat with straps you can cinch to the picnic-table bench might work better.

Even in the absence of a picnic table, a portable seat is still a good idea. When Quinn was less than two, we camped at a primitive site near Winter

Park, Colorado. At mealtimes, he sat on the ground in a plastic booster with a snap-on tray. And when your toddler is contained at dinnertime, you can relax for at least two minutes.

COOKWARE: THE KITCHEN GEAR YOU NEED TO FEED THE FAMILY

Preparing a meal in the woods can be tricky but not insurmountable. And maybe it's because you're starved by the time you sit down to eat, but even a PB&J eaten alfresco somehow tastes better. The key to success is to plan your menu (see ideas on page 89) and really think through how you'll make each dish: Visualize your campground prep (e.g., you'll need a spatula for flipping pancakes, a pot and strainer for pasta, a small cutting board for dicing peppers, and so on).

For some, our family included, going gourmet with a babbling brook at your tableside and a canopy of trees overhead is half the fun. I once insisted we try making pizza while camping. I made the dough from scratch at home, then we rolled it out with a wine bottle at the campsite. (Now, if I'd thought through the camp prep, I would have packed my rolling pin.) Using tinfoil and a pot lid, we created an impromptu pizza oven. After completely scorching the first pie, we got the heat right, and it was darn tasty. And we were eating freshly baked pizza in the woods!

When it comes to cookware, if you want to make something in the backcountry, there's probably a device for it. There are s'more makers, waffle griddles, and pie irons for grilled sandwiches. The list is endless. Personal preference will determine what cookware you need, if any, as will your menu. If you are the ascetic type, all you really need is a fire and a stick for your hot dogs.

Camp Stove

While backpackers perform balancing acts with boiling pots of reconstituted chicken Alfredo over tiny stoves perched on rocks, car campers can bring out

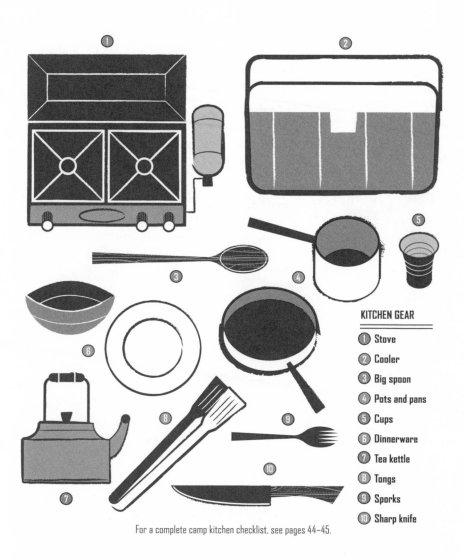

KITCHEN GEAR

1. Stove
2. Cooler
3. Big spoon
4. Pots and pans
5. Cups
6. Dinnerware
7. Tea kettle
8. Tongs
9. Sporks
10. Sharp knife

For a complete camp kitchen checklist, see pages 44–45.

the big guns: the two-burner, table-mounted camp stove. Your pancakes can be fluffing up on one burner while the bacon is sizzling on the next. Most of these stoves run on one-pound tanks of propane, which is probably the most sensible fuel for car camping because it's relatively safe and easy to use. If you don't like monkeying around with matches, consider a stove with a push-button electric ignition. When shopping for a stove, check out the flame-adjusting dials for ease of use.

At the top end, Brunton has camp stoves with two 15,000 Btu burners and extruded aluminum exteriors that fold up like a Maxwell Smart briefcase. At around $450, this kind of camp stove might be nicer than your stove at home. Camp Chef offers models that combine a range and an oven, if freshly baked banana-nut muffins are on your menu. There are even camp stoves that literally come with a kitchen sink.

SMART TIP A family could probably get away with one small propane canister for cooking over a weekend trip, but you don't want to run out of fuel before the eggs are fried. Just in case, bring a backup. Even if you do run out, cans of propane can be found nearly anywhere—camping stores, gas stations, even grocery stores.

More reasonably priced models abound, with the classic forest-green, two-burner Coleman stove starting around $70. Even with such a simple stove, which is all we've ever had, you can make plenty of delicious camp meals. Maybe all you require of a stove is boiling water for packets of oatmeal and chicken noodle soup, in which case a basic, single-burner camp stove will do.

Cookware

We have a battered aluminum teakettle and some cooking pots that I inherited from my parents' camping days. They're lightweight and durable and nostalgic of the seventies, but because they're not a set, they don't nest together well. If you buy modern, camp-specific cookware, you can get space-efficient pots and pans with handles that are removable, transferrable, or that fold away. Look for lids that double as frying pans, mesh bags for air-drying dishes, and rugged stuff sacks that can be used as makeshift sinks. GSI Outdoors has sets where the utensils fit inside the cups, which fit inside the bowls, which fit inside small pots, and so on. Some sets come color-coded so family members know which plate, cup, and utensil belongs to them.

If you plan to cook over a fire, be sure to bring an old pot. The bottom will be black with soot by the time your water boils.

Cooking Utensils

Depending on your menu, you'll need big spoons for stirring, long-handled tongs for removing foil packets from the fire, a whisk for the scrambled eggs. You can buy dedicated camping utensils that are lightweight and scaled-down in size for backpackers. But if you're car camping, it's just as easy to raid your own kitchen drawers. And if you forget the metal spatula for grilling the New York strip steaks, you'll be flipping them with a salad fork. We've done precisely that, and the steaks were magnificent.

SMART TIP An essential, affordable, must-have camp kitchen gadget is the pot lifter (also called a pot grabber). Pot handles can be hot or even break off over time. Pot lifters clamp onto the lip of a pot like a pair of fitted pliers, allowing you to safely pick up a pot of boiling water. No oven mitts required.

To transport your eight-inch chef's knife (and steak knives, if you're bringing those), fashion a sleeve out of cardboard and packing tape. If you leave sharp knives loose and unprotected in your big plastic box of cookware, you're asking to lose a fingertip.

Camp Kits

When it comes to your camp dinnerware, you can certainly go the high-tech route. We've always taken the dirtbag approach. Our camp cupboard is a mishmash of reusable plastic bowls from Target, slightly tarnished silver

Garage sales are a great place to pick up old cutlery for camping. Repurposing flatware helps reduce waste, lessening the environmental impact of your camping adventure. Plus, if you only paid 30 cents for a fork, you won't mind if the kids use it to scratch their names in the dirt.

dessert forks from a garage sale, my old Girl Scout mess kit, and decades-old miniature spatula and serving spoon from EMS. Our collection works fine, but it's a bit cumbersome.

The advantage of going with plates, bowls, and utensils designed for camping is that they are lightweight, durable, space efficient, and come in nifty carrying cases. Drinking cups are designed to work as measuring cups. Eating bowls might have accompanying lids for storage. Utensils stack neatly and tuck into fabric sleeves that roll up for transport. Spork systems—utensils that combine spoon, fork, and knife—minimize your cutlery needs. Sea to Summit has bowls and mugs that collapse down to the size of a Frisbee and fit into the company's camp plate. You can even get telescoping sporks and foldable chopsticks.

Disposable Dinnerware

If you're just sticking your pinkie toe into the waters of family camping, or maybe you're just looking to simplify, you might consider using disposable paper plates and plastic utensils. It's more economical than buying a set of spiffy camp kits, and cleanup is virtually nonexistent. You just pile all the plates and utensils in a garbage bag and drop the bag in the campground Dumpster.

If disposable dinnerware gets you and your kids out into the woods, that's a good thing. That said, do you really want all those plastic forks to end up in the landfill? Or worse yet, in the Pacific Ocean's Trash Vortex? I will say no more.

The Camp Kitchen

Most campgrounds have picnic tables, so you don't need to stack your pots in the dirt like you would if you were backpacking in the deep woods. But if you're the kind of person who alphabetizes your spice jars, you might consider a camp kitchen, which is a collapsible system for organizing the pantry and stove. When assembled, there's a surface for the stove, a counter surface for your ingredients and food prep, shelves built into a canvas cabinet that zips closed, even a paper-towel holder. Kelty, Cabela's, and Coleman make camp-kitchen systems.

If you don't want another twenty pounds of gear or don't feel like spending upwards of $150 on a camp kitchen, you can stow pantry items in giant, heavy-duty Rubbermaid tubs. In camp, you can just use the picnic table to spread out your kitchen gear.

Cooking Accessories: Gee-Whiz Gadgets

So you thought the beauty of camping was its inherent simplicity, right? Roasted hot dogs followed by toasted Jet-Puffs? Well, when it comes to camp cooking, it's possible to stock up on more gadgets than Rachael Ray could shake a marshmallow stick at. Just suppose, for a minute, you couldn't find a stick in the woods. You'd be wise to bring along a six-capacity, chrome-plated wiener-roasting stick with inverted tines so your franks don't slip into the fire. Rome Outdoor Cookware makes such a thing. It also has a steel basket device for roasting three s'mores over the fire (again, you probably thought you just needed a thin branch). In fact, Rome makes a metal marshmallow roasting stick . . . shaped like a stick.

SMART TIP Back home, keep all the bits and pieces of camping gear, from pots and utensils to headlamps and poop shovels, in your big plastic tubs in the garage. It'll make the job of packing go more smoothly if everything is in one place.

You can find all manner of pie irons for grilling sandwiches, corn bread, waffles, hot dogs, and desserts. They come in heavy-duty cast iron and have long handles so you can stick the iron right in the fire for an alfresco panini or French toast. Rome makes a complete line of pie irons for campers.

COMPOSTABLE DINNERWARE: EATING CORN ON CORN

Remember the edible candy teacups shaped like little yellow flowers in Willy Wonka's chocolate room? Eating corn on the cob on a plate made of corn sounds a little like something the crazy candy man would have dreamed up. If you're not ready to invest in state-of-the-art camp cookware, but you also don't want to use environmentally unconscionable plastic forks, plates, and cups, compostable dinnerware might split the difference.

There are cups, plates, and utensils made from starches (like corn and potato) or from sugarcane fiber (a by-product of sugar production). They are designed to decompose in commercial composting facilities and possibly in backyard compost piles. Though I've had a compostable spoon in my compost bin for months, and it's still entirely intact. These products tend to be chemical-free, so when they do break down, they can transform—along with banana peels and past-due salsa—into a nutrient-rich fertilizer that's great for the garden. Compostable tableware can assuage the guilt of one-time use, but it's expensive compared with plastic.

But here's the real sticky wicket: if you don't actually compost these products and simply toss them in the trash instead, you've wasted your money and neutralized your earth-friendly efforts. Like other organic matter (apple cores, coffee grounds, old leaves), compostable tableware needs oxygen and moisture to biodegrade. By design, landfills are virtually oxygen and moisture-free. When organics are entombed in a landfill, they may not degrade for decades. And if they do decompose in a landfill, they release methane, a greenhouse gas twenty-one times more potent than carbon dioxide. According to the EPA, the United States generates thirty-four million tons of food waste. In 2009, a whopping thirty-three million tons was thrown away, ending up in either landfills or incinerators. As a result, landfills are the country's second largest human-related source of methane.[2]

Whether organic materials like compostable plates will decompose in a landfill in our lifetime is debatable. In 1974, Dr. William Rathje, a professor of archaeology at the University of Arizona, undertook a research study called the Garbage Project. It was essentially an archaeological dig of landfills. During those early digs and in subsequent excavations, Dr. Rathje discovered legible newspapers from the 1930s, decade-old carrot tips and onion parings, and a perfectly preserved twenty-five-year-old head of lettuce. If lettuce doesn't break down, a hard spoon of sugarcane doesn't have much of a chance. In his book *Rubbish!: The Archaeology of Garbage*, Dr. Rathje says that "[Landfills] are not vast composters; rather, they are vast mummifiers."[3]

So, if you go the compostable-fork route when you're camping, you need to collect the compostables, cart them home, and get them into the compost. Campers are good stewards of the land. As such, you should do everything in your power to get that fork back to Mother Earth.

If you must have proper toast with your tea, for a few bucks Coghlan's sells a metal cage device that suspends bread over your camp stove's flame. The only toasted bread I've had while camping was a slice I tossed in the grease after cooking up bacon on the camp stove—and it was perfectly tasty.

If your menu tends toward Asian cooking (sushi, perhaps?), Snow Peak makes a rice cooker for campers. How about a portable pressure cooker for that white-bean-and-pancetta stew? GSI Outdoors makes one that weighs less than five pounds. Or maybe you don't need any of that at all. Maybe you just need a stick to roast a bratwurst over the campfire.

Coolers

The joy of car camping is that you don't have to squeeze tiny packets of freeze-dried food into your backpack just to get a little sustenance. You can bring

CAMP KITCHEN CHECKLIST

- ☐ Camp kitchen
- ☐ Camp stove
- ☐ Fuel
- ☐ Pots
- ☐ Pans
- ☐ Skillet
- ☐ Grill rack
- ☐ Cutting board
- ☐ Sharp knife
- ☐ Measuring cup
- ☐ Measuring spoons
- ☐ Spatula
- ☐ Big spoon
- ☐ Long-handled tongs
- ☐ Strainer
- ☐ Plates
- ☐ Bowls
- ☐ Cups
- ☐ Insulated coffee cups
- ☐ Water bottles
- ☐ Utensils
- ☐ Marshmallow sticks
- ☐ Corkscrew
- ☐ Bottle opener
- ☐ Pot lifter
- ☐ Aluminum foil

a big old cooler filled with steaks and gallons of milk. We've found that for a family of five, having not one, but *two* coolers helps keep us organized. One cooler for food; one for drinks. If your kids are content with water and you don't love beer as much as I do, you could easily get away with just one cooler.

Look for insulated coolers with hard plastic or even steel sides, rather than soft-sided coolers. They'll keep your eggs and bacon colder for longer, and they can double as extra seats. For a price, you can find coolers that promise to keep ice up to five days in 90-degree heat. Make sure the lid is easy to open and close, because with growing kids in your clan, you'll be in and out of the cooler continuously. Wheels that can handle rough terrain are a bonus.

Drinking Cups

Any old reusable plastic cups will do for the kids. Our camp cups are a collection of reusable kid cups saved from restaurant meals. They also work nicely as sand toys. Of course, the major camp cookware companies offer a host of clever

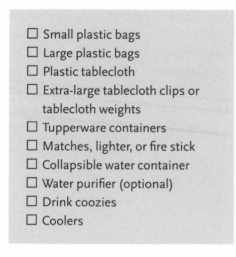

- Small plastic bags
- Large plastic bags
- Plastic tablecloth
- Extra-large tablecloth clips or tablecloth weights
- Tupperware containers
- Matches, lighter, or fire stick
- Collapsible water container
- Water purifier (optional)
- Drink coozies
- Coolers

SMART TIP Bring along tablecloth weights or extra-large clips for the picnic table to keep your plastic tablecloth from flying away in the wind.

cup options. There are mugs in baked enamel, titanium, stainless steel, and BPA-free plastic. MSR and GSI Outdoors have insulated, color-coded cups shaped sort of like a rounded trapezoid, which allows four cups to fit together inside a pot. And they come with sipping lids.

For your morning java, an insulated cup is key. Remember, there's no microwave to warm it up. We bring along basic, insulated to-go mugs to keep breakfast tea and après-dinner cocoa hot.

For your cabernet sauvignon, you can either rough it by sipping out of your coffee mug, which somehow feels like camping to me, or you can get fancy with a stemless, stainless-steel wineglass. You can find these at GSI Outdoors. They also have rugged stainless-steel wineglasses with stems that pop off and stow inside the cup. But a wineglass with a stem perched on a rock that's surrounded by a posse of kids hopped up on s'mores sounds like a recipe for spilled wine. And that's something to cry over.

Dutch Ovens

One-dish meals make sense for camping, and the Dutch oven is an ideal tool for simmering a great big pot of chili or gumbo. You can make just about anything in a Dutch oven, from pizza and burritos to corn bread and peach cobbler. The Dutch oven can be used over a camp stove, charcoal, or hot campfire coals. Camp Chef and Lodge Cast Iron make Dutch ovens that are already seasoned and designed for camping.

Look for models with stubby little legs to stand over the coals, as well as flanged lids (ones with lips on them) so coals won't roll off when you pile them on top. Most lids reverse for use as skillets. A ten-inch oven should suffice for most families. Dutch ovens weigh in at twenty to thirty pounds, so you won't want to lug one into the backcountry—or drop one on your toes.

Water Purifiers

See "Stream Water: Drink Smart," page 223.

SOFTWEAR: THE CLOTHES YOU NEED TO KEEP WARM, COOL, AND DRY

Once upon a time, camping folks dressed like lumberjacks: sturdy jeans, heavy plaid flannel shirts, Timberland work boots. Maybe even a red union suit with a drop seat at the rear. Times have changed, and this is good news. Nowadays, the clothes you can wear while camping are softer, lighter, more flattering, and higher performing. When it comes to kids, you'll find the same technical flourishes in their clothing, but with bright colors and adorable prints.

Modern garments wick away moisture and dry quickly. High-tech shell jackets shed water, yet they still let your body breathe. Pants transform into shorts. Some garments are specifically engineered to protect your skin from the damaging rays of the sun. Even the lowly sock has become considerably high-tech in the twenty-first century.

Base Layers: Go High-Tech

When summer camping, you'll likely spend most of your day in shorts and a T-shirt. But even in August, temperatures dip as the sun goes down, so you'll want a pair of long underwear just in case. For camping in fall and spring,

CAMP CLOTHES

1. Base layers
2. Vest
3. Wickable T-shirt
4. Fleece top and convertible pants
5. Shell jacket
6. Sun hat
7. Boots
8. Socks

For complete softwear and footwear checklists, see pages 54 and 56.

you may even want that base layer during the day. If you still have those heavy cotton long johns with the tiny waffle grid, it's time to upgrade.

Synthetic fabrics like polyester, nylon, or polypropylene are comfortable,

GEARING UP

lightweight, and high performing. If you prefer a natural fiber, merino wool is a good choice, though wool doesn't dry as quickly as synthetic fabrics. SmartWool and Icebreaker have lightweight, high-performing merino wool T-shirts and base layers that are surprisingly itch-free.

Unlike those '70s-era cotton long undies, which trap moisture and hang on to it, today's next-to-skin layers wick moisture and dry quickly. Your next-to-skin layer is really a moisture-management tool. As you *schvitz* under the weight of a forty-pound toddler, these fabrics pull that moisture away from your body and through the fabric, where it evaporates quickly. For kids, who not only sweat but also splash themselves in ponds and spill apple juice down their shirts, a fabric that dries quickly is critical.

Many modern base layers also come with antimicrobial properties designed to keep you smelling fresh as a daisy. At the very least, the stink-fighting technology can buy you a few more days of wear.

Sleepwear: Nighttime Is Jammie Time

Your base layer can double as pajamas at night—if they are clean. You don't want to dirty up your sleeping bag with pants caked in mud. And you never want to sleep in clothing smeared with food, because it can attract bears. From my backpacking days, I've become conditioned to sleeping in long johns or the next day's T-shirt. But for kids, there's no reason not to pack their favorite footed pj's. They are soft, comfy, familiar, and can signal that the bedtime routine is at hand. Plus, most kids' clothes are teeny, and you're not so worried about space because you're car camping. So bring the jammies.

Second Layer: Get Fleeced

Layering is the key to staying comfortable in the outdoors. Weather can vary greatly from early morning to midday to stargazing time. Activity level also affects temperature regulation. You'll be toasty when you're hiking up a steep trail; you'll cool down as soon as you stop for a snack break on a windy rock outcrop.

SMART TIP

Take a page from Johnny Cash and dress in black. You're in the woods. It's dirty. Forget the lights and whites; pack dark clothing instead. The exception is on hikes, when it's helpful to dress kids in bright colors, which makes them easier to spot.

Over your base layer, you'll need a midweight fleece top and bottom layer for insulation. Fleece clothing, made from polyester—sometimes even from recycled plastic bottles—is lightweight, breathable, and quick drying. Fleece is also ubiquitous. You can find stacks of fleece pullovers at Target and Old Navy. But choose a high-end fleece garment from Patagonia or The North Face, and it'll last for years. If you have more than one child—or younger nieces and nephews waiting in the wings—it makes sense to go with a good quality fleece for the hand-me-down factor. All three of my kids have worn the Patagonia zip-up fleece jacket I found at a garage sale years ago. It still looks brand-new.

You can also use a lightweight, low-profile down jacket as an insulating layer. These jackets are cozy and compressible, though not as affordable as fleece.

Shell Layer: Battling the Elements

To complete the layering package, you'll need an outer shell jacket. Whether you ever pull it out of your pack or not depends on the weather. But each camper in the family should be prepared with a weatherproof outer layer to protect them from wind, rain, and snow. You won't ever plan to camp in the snow, but twice in Yellowstone—where it is said there are only two seasons, winter and August—I've encountered summer snows. Those rubbery raincoats that make kids look like ducks and ladybugs are cute, but they're not terribly functional for camping.

The best (and most expensive) shells are waterproof and breathable. They'll keep you dry in a downpour while letting moisture escape from your body. Without breathability, your inner layers will get soggy from perspiration. And

GEARING UP

a wet camper is a chilled camper. If you're camping in drier climates, you might go with a more affordable water-resistant, breathable shell.

SMART TIP

Use dedicated cleaning detergents like Nikwax and Sport-Wash to launder waterproof-breathable clothing. Garden-variety laundry detergents can leave a residue that will negatively impact the water resiliency of technical rain gear. Never use fabric softeners or dryer sheets with high-tech garments; they can also mitigate the performance of a waterproof jacket.

Rain-worthy shells achieve waterproofness in two basic ways: laminate technology and coatings. With laminates, waterproof materials are sandwiched into a garment's fabric. Coatings are sprayed onto the fabric's exterior. Although laminates are more breathable and more technical, with their taped seams and clever low-profile zippers, coated rain-wear is generally more affordable. Kids grow out of jackets at an alarming rate. Go with a pocketbook-friendly rain shell with a waterproof coating, rather than a costly laminated model.

We also like to pack lightweight rain pants. The rain rarely deters our kids from playing outside, and the full-body approach helps keep the warming layers dry and cozy.

Hands and Heads

Your mother always said that you lose 75 percent of your body heat through your head. Your mom was wrong, but you should listen to her anyway. You do lose some body heat through the head (more like 10 percent), so a hat will undoubtedly help keep you warm. Even when camping in summer, bring along a warm fleece hat and lightweight gloves. Mornings and evenings can be cool enough to necessitate these wintertime accessories. And in the middle of the night, the air in the tent can be downright chilly. If burrowing into a sleeping bag on a cold night gives you a case of claustrophobia, wearing a hat while sleeping is the perfect solution.

When it's sunny, be sure to plop a sun hat on each child's noggin. Floppy hats with wide brims or legionnaires' caps with neck-shading flaps at the back deliver the best protection from the sun. Even a baseball cap is better than no hat at all. REI, Outdoor Research, Sunday Afternoons, and Columbia have great kids' hats, with bright colors, whimsical prints, and lots of sun protection. If you're looking for a sun hat that will actually stay put on a baby's head, try the brimmed hats with neck flaps from Flap Happy.

Multifunctional Headgear: Modern Do-Rag

The elements encountered while camping—wind, dirt, sun—can turn an innocent case of bed head into Medusa on a bad-hair day. I've always packed a bandana for covering up my rat's nest around the campsite. A modern twist on the bandana is called a Buff. It's a thin polyester tube that, when twisted and folded, can be worn a dozen different ways. It's a cap, a headband, hair band, a do-rag, and a neckerchief all in one. My kids love wearing them pirate-style.

Temperature Regulation

When you're outdoors in changeable weather, you'll find you're too hot one minute, too cold the next. You can be peeling off layers like an onion but still be unable to achieve equilibrium on par with Baby Bear's oatmeal.

Beyond layering, there are several ways you can fine-tune your temperature control. Start by bringing along a fleece or down vest, which keeps your core warm while allowing ventilation at the arms. It's ideal for times when a full jacket is too much.

Zip-off pants are a great choice when you head out on a hike on a crisp morning. When the sun starts baking, simply zip off the pant legs, and voilà, you're wearing shorts. Look for jackets with "pit zips," zippers at the armpits that allow for copious ventilation where you need it most.

Shorts and T-shirts: Beyond Cotton

Your children's dressers are likely filled with dozens of cotton T-shirts and shorts. And they'll do fine for camping. Cotton is comfortable, and most young kids don't sweat very much. But cotton is a hydrophilic material, meaning it loves water. If those cotton shorts get wet while Junior is fording a river, they won't dry very quickly. You're better off with outdoor garments made with synthetic fabrics like nylon and polyester, which are designed to wick away moisture and dry quickly. Look for outdoor-specific shorts and shirts from The North Face, Columbia, Royal Robbins, ExOfficio, and Mountain Hardwear.

Sun Protection: Beyond Sunscreen

If your clan is full of fair-skinned, freckly, green-eyed Celts like me, or you're camping at high elevation or near the equator, you might consider clothing with Ultraviolet Protection Factor, or UPF. It's the SPF of the fabric world.

Polyester fabric is naturally better than cotton at deflecting the sun's rays, so that's a good first step. Garments designed specifically to block the sun's rays often use polyester, but they also employ special dyes and treatments and are constructed with tightly woven fibers. Most mainstream outdoor-clothing companies have UPF clothing in their lines. Columbia in particular has a robust collection of UPF shorts and shirts designed for kids. Companies like Sun Precautions make clothing exclusively for sun protection.

Socks

The first step to keeping feet warm, dry, and blister-free is to abandon the baggy, white cotton tube socks. Use them for sock puppets. Cotton is infamous for sucking up moisture, drying slowly, and leaving you with cold feet. And feet sure do sweat. According to the California Podiatric Medical

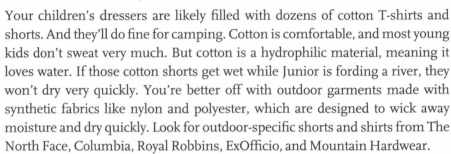

Association, each foot has 250,000 sweat glands, which on average produce enough sweat each day to fill an eggcup.[4]

To deal with sweaty feet, little campers need a good pair of wool or synthetic socks designed for active outdoor use. Lightweight hiking socks work best. Look for socks with soft, comfortable synthetic materials like acrylic and polyester, which provide great insulation, dry quickly, and are durable. Many socks add Lycra for stretch, Coolmax for wicking moisture, and nylon for abrasion resistance. Thorlos makes great synthetic socks that stand up over time.

Some sock makers, like Lorpen and Wigwam, will combine a touch of merino wool with synthetic materials for extra warmth. Generally speaking, wool is better than cotton at keeping you warm, even when wet. But wool on its own doesn't dry as easily as synthetic materials, plus it's less durable and notoriously itchy. SmartWool has figured out how to scrub off the prickly bits from a thread of yarn so you can have the warmth of wool in a sock without the itchy-scratchies.

To avoid rifling through mounds of clothes to find a tiny pair of socks, keep socks and underwear in a small mesh bag. The bags designed for laundering fine lingerie work nicely for this. Also bring a laundry bag or plastic bag for dirty clothes. This way you can keep them separate from the clean clothes during the trip, and when you get home, you can dump the bag right into the hamper.

You might be surprised at the level of technology that goes into sock design. A well-designed hiking sock might have stretchy panels around the arch to keep the sock in place, mesh zones to enhance ventilation, and reinforced cushioning at the heel and under the ball of the foot to help prevent the hot spots that come from impact and shear.

FOOTWEAR: THE ESSENTIAL SHOE COLLECTION FOR CAMPERS

For a rafting trip down the Colorado River, in lieu of my usual flip-flops, I pulled out an old pair of strap sandals. It seemed prudent. At our first stop,

I walked about twenty yards down a gravelly trail before I realized my shoes were rapidly disintegrating. (They had, after all, been sitting idly in my closet for about a decade.) My son Aidan ran after me waving a rubber sole. Luckily I'd packed an extra pair of water shoes for Aidan, so I was able to usurp his brand-new Tevas. (Fortuitously, we have roughly the same size foot.)

The point here is to be prepared. I caution in this book about not overpacking, but you sure don't want to get caught up a river without a sandal. When hiking boots start to pinch, you'll want to slip into some sneakers. And when the little stinkers immerse their feet in a stream, sturdy sandals are a good backup.

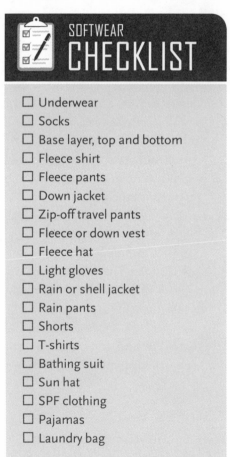

SOFTWEAR CHECKLIST

- ☐ Underwear
- ☐ Socks
- ☐ Base layer, top and bottom
- ☐ Fleece shirt
- ☐ Fleece pants
- ☐ Down jacket
- ☐ Zip-off travel pants
- ☐ Fleece or down vest
- ☐ Fleece hat
- ☐ Light gloves
- ☐ Rain or shell jacket
- ☐ Rain pants
- ☐ Shorts
- ☐ T-shirts
- ☐ Bathing suit
- ☐ Sun hat
- ☐ SPF clothing
- ☐ Pajamas
- ☐ Laundry bag

Hiking Boots or Light Hikers

Hiking boots are the de rigueur footwear for campers who hike. If your idea of the perfect camping trip is never venturing farther from the campsite than the Porta-John, you can get away with sandals and sneakers. But if you're going to hit the trail with kids, you all need good sturdy shoes with knobby treads for traction and heavy-duty uppers for protection against sharp rocks and sticks.

If you're not committed to boots, consider light hikers, or hiking shoes, which are cut lower on the ankle. They are a bit less substantial than full-on hiking boots, but they're still supportive and feature rugged soles that grip the trail. I can tell you my son Aidan wished he had on hiking boots the time he ran through a prickly pear cactus while wearing sandals.

SMART TIP Save some cash by seeking out pre-owned hiking boots. Cozy up to an outdoorsy family with kids a little older than your kids. Or more to the point, kids who have feet a little bigger than your kids' feet. Unlike sneakers, hiking boots and shoes are durable enough to last through several kids.

It's not easy to fork over the dough for pint-sized hiking boots when you know the kids will outgrow them by the end of the summer, and Walmart sells sneakers for ten bucks. But consider this: when hiking, children slip five times more often than their parents. That's a totally made-up statistic, but I can report anecdotally that it's true of my kids. And when kids skid and fall, they skin their knees and grate their palms—which in turn makes them cry at earsplitting volumes. You'll wish you'd forked over the dough.

Another benefit of good hiking boots or shoes is the waterproof factor. When I was young, we waterproofed our boots by first sliding our feet into empty Wonder Bread bags. It made the boots waterproof but decidedly not breathable. Most decent hiking-boot models are at least water-resistant. If you're hiking around in the rain or your kids like to jump in puddles (and all kids like to jump in puddles), you'll be glad the boots shed water.

Before you take a long hike on a camping trip, be sure to break in new hiking boots or shoes by either wearing them around the house for a few days or going on short local hikes.

Sneakers

Hiking boots just don't have the slipper-like comfort of your sneakers. After a long hike, you'll be glad to slide your feet into a comfy pair of tennis shoes.

And for kids, sneakers are a good backup in case their hiking boots start to rub them the wrong way.

Sandals

Sandals are great for hanging around the campsite and letting your tootsies breathe on a hot day. They're also handy for slipping on and off when you're in and out of the tent every five minutes. If sandals get wet when kids are chucking rocks in a lake, they'll dry out quicker than a soaked sneaker. For running around the campsite and wading in water, sandals that strap securely onto the foot are better than flip-flops or slide-ons. Keen, Chaco, and Teva all make sandals for active campers.

Water Shoes

These little slip-on rubber shoes are perfect for walking around in a shallow, slow-moving stream with a rocky bottom. If you're camping near a beach, water shoes are great for playing on a pebbled-covered shoreline. When sea creatures like spiny urchins and pinching crabs lurk in the depths, kids will be more willing to wade in if they're wearing water shoes. Speedo and Tuga make slip-on water shoes, but you can also find cheap pairs at Target.

Camp Booties

Even in summer, the mercury can dive at night. That's when you want

SMART TIP Put a pair of slip-on sandals or flip-flops at the door of the tent for midnight pee breaks. Nobody, especially a six-year-old, wants to be tying laces in the dead of night.

FOOTWEAR CHECKLIST

- ☐ Hiking boots or light hikers
- ☐ Sneakers
- ☐ Sandals with straps
- ☐ Flip-flops
- ☐ Water shoes
- ☐ Camp booties

to break out the camp booties. These down-filled slippers with relatively hard soles are like little sleeping bags for your feet, just the thing for sitting by the fire and puttering around the campsite. They are also ideal for backpacking and for wearing inside a hut, if you were ever to take the kids on a hut trip.

PART TWO

IN THE FIELD

In a small backyard, by a squat stone fence,
Five little ducks pitch five duck tents.
"All five up!" five proud ducks cheer.
Ducks fill tents with camping gear.
Lanterns, pillows, sleeping bags,
Fishing poles—brand-new with tags.

—*Duck Tents* by Lynne Berry

Chapter Three

THE CAMPSITE

Outside our tent I can see
gray spiders spinning silver,
looping silky lines
through smoky wisps
of campfire, coffee steam,
and early morning mist.

—Toasting Marshmallows: Camping Poems
by Kristine O'Connell George

Once the gear is procured, the campsite chosen, the menus planned and prepped, you're ready to get out there and camp. This, my friends, is the fun part.

When you arrive at a campground, the first order of business is to make camp. Try to think of setting up camp as an activity, not a chore. Enlist kids to help unload the car. Sleeping bags, pillows, and sleeping pads are all light enough for even the youngest campers to carry. When my two boys were nine and six, they insisted on carrying a heavy bundle of shrink-wrapped firewood from the car (they pushed it, they dragged it, they rolled it). That's when I knew that camp setup could be an integral part of the overall camping adventure.

In addition to advice on setting up camp, this section covers the campfire, campsite etiquette, and breaking down camp. None of this, I promise you,

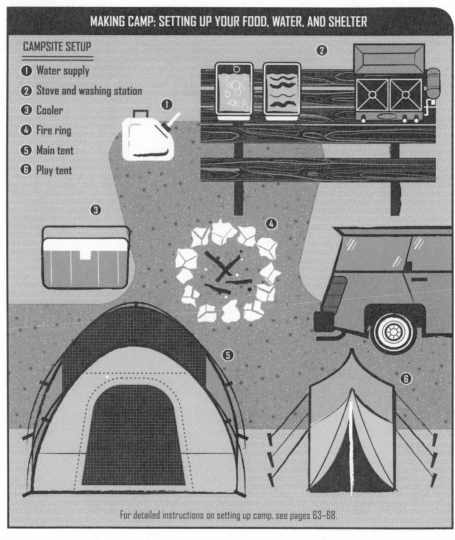

MAKING CAMP: SETTING UP YOUR FOOD, WATER, AND SHELTER

CAMPSITE SETUP

1. Water supply
2. Stove and washing station
3. Cooler
4. Fire ring
5. Main tent
6. Play tent

For detailed instructions on setting up camp, see pages 63-68.

is rocket science. But over the years, I've learned a few tricks of the camping trade from campers more adept than I am, as well as through my own trial and error. Consider this: For years, when it came time to break camp, I would spent a good quarter hour on my hands and knees with a little dustpan and whisk broom, trying to remove the dirt off my tent floor. I knew instantly there was a better way when I saw a friend zip open the door of his tent and shake out the dirt in mere seconds. It was a true "Aha!" moment.

MAKING CAMP: THE SETUP

Remember that prodigious pile of gear you crammed into the car? Now it's time to unload it all and set up camp. Ideally you've arrived early enough in the day that there are no ill-tempered campers in your ranks, and you still have plenty of daylight.

If you have a reservation, then you simply need to find your allotted site. Scout it out and envision your alfresco living arrangements. If you're in an established campground, your general configuration is pretty much determined for you. Most campgrounds have permanent fire rings, picnic tables, and tent pads. You'll still need to consider where to set up the camp kitchen and cleaning station, screen house (if you have one), and camp chairs.

Given a Choice: Finding the Perfect Spot

Arrive late to a campground in the busy season without a reservation in hand, and you'll probably get skunked on a site. But if the campground isn't busy, walk-in campers have the luxury of choosing a campsite on the spot. In this situation, a little reconnaissance is in order. Look for a site that is roomy, provides some privacy from nearby campsites, and is within a short walking distance—though not sniffing distance—from the bathrooms.

Choose a site that's not too far from the campground's water pump or spigot. You'll be collecting water for cooking, cleaning, and washing up, which is to say, you'll be using a fair amount of water. Water is heavy and it sloshes around when you carry it, so you want your water source relatively close by.

Especially in the dog days of summer, choose a site that has some trees for shade. Ideally you can get a spot that's sunny in the morning and shady in the afternoon. Shade is critical if you have nappers in your brood. A tent that's been baking in the sun all day is like a nylon sauna. You want kids rested, not roasted.

If you're camping in the backcountry where there are no established sites, be sure to set up camp at least two hundred feet from streams, lakes, and ponds to protect water sources from contamination.

Safety First: Consider Potential Hazards

When our kids were little, we intentionally didn't camp near rivers. Although a stream rushing past your tent is picturesque and soothing when you're tucked in your sleeping bag, the danger it poses isn't worth the parental angst. An acquaintance of mine recalls fishing with his parents as a kid. His mom was afraid he'd fall in the river, so they tied him to a nearby tree.

SMART TIP

When camping with babies and toddlers, bring along a portable crib so you can set up camp without worrying that your little ones are chewing on rocks and eating dirt.

Like a dog on a short leash. It may have been effective, but I can't in good conscience recommend this.

Especially if your tribe comprises toddlers and babies, or you don't want to watch your children every minute, don't camp near rivers, reservoirs, lakes, or ponds. If you do choose to camp near water—and kids love to camp near water because there's nothing better than chucking rocks and hearing the resulting *kerplunk*—adults need to take turns providing dedicated supervision.

Other potential campsite hazards to consider are cliffs, steep hills, and rocky outcrops. If there's a giant boulder nearby, kids will climb up it. You need to assess your children's ages, personalities, and the potential risk of the natural playgrounds that a campground creates.

Tent Placement: Flat, High, and Smooth

Most campsites will have an established tent pad, which is a big square of flat dirt, usually framed by railroad ties or logs. This durable, level surface helps

SMART TIP If high winds are in the forecast and you've staked your tent in loose soil or sand, carefully place smooth, heavy rocks in the corners of your tent.

reduce the environmental impact of busy campgrounds because the same spot is used time and again.

Usually tent pads are pretty level. But it only takes the slightest angle to make sleeping on the ground tricky. If the surface underneath your tent is on a gentle slope, you'll want to set up your sleeping bags parallel to the incline so your heads are higher than your feet. Just pretend you're in one of those reclining hospital beds.

More than once, we've pitched our tent on a slight hill. But only once did we set up our bags perpendicular to the incline. This is a mistake. During the night, we rolled downhill like hot dogs, leaving us all in a heap in the morning.

If you're camping in a primitive campground or in the backcountry, finding a flat spot is the holy grail of tent placement. Look for an area that's relatively free of rocks, especially sharp ones. Think about the princess and all the trouble she had with that pea. Choose a spot that's on relatively high ground. Pitch your tent in a low spot, and you'll be sleeping in a puddle if it rains.

Door Placement

Once you've found a suitable spot for pitching your tent, you'll want to think about the best way to orient the door. Consider the ease of entry and exit. You don't want to be constantly circling the tent to get inside it. But you also don't want the door to be facing a pit toilet or a busy campground road.

Think feng shui. Thoughtful door placement can afford you an added degree of privacy. What do you want to look at when you first open the tent door in the morning? We always orient the door toward the best view.

Pitching the Tent

Once you've found your tent spot and figured out your door orientation, spread out your tarp, or ground cloth. If you encounter rain, it's critical that the tarp is slightly smaller than the tent floor. Otherwise, any pieces of tarp sticking out beyond the tent walls will serve as funnels for rainwater to flow between the tarp and the tent's underside, where it can then seep inside. You want any precipitation to flow under the tarp and soak back into Mother Earth. So, when you position the tarp, make sure it is fully covered by your tent. If your tarp is larger than your tent floor, neatly fold under any excess.

Next, roll out the tent and assemble it according to the manufacturer's directions, which you followed when you did the dry run in the backyard. (You did that, right?) It helps to assemble all the poles first, thread them into the tent's tiny pole sleeves, and erect the whole shebang *before* you stake the corners down.

Be sure to have kids help set up the tent. Mine love putting together the shock-corded collapsible poles. The snapping of aluminum and the simple creation of an enormously long pole is highly gratifying to them. The more invested kids are in the setup process, the more they'll get out of the camping experience, including a boost to their self-confidence. The contingency plan: if your children's attention span runs out, bring along crayons and paper, Frisbees and Nerf footballs. This will keep your children occupied while you finish making camp.

Use fluorescent or brightly colored ribbon to tie bows on the tent's guylines. Place them at your child's eye level. This will help prevent kids from tripping on the guylines.

Sleeping Bags and Pads

Once the tent is up and staked down, it's time to feather your nest. Don't wait until bedtime to roll out your sleeping pads and sleeping bags. Sleep-

Set up your sleeping bags so your feet are near the door. Otherwise, little people with dirty feet will be walking on your pillow.

ing bags work best if the insulation has time to fluff up. Make a plan as a family to decide who's going to sleep next to whom, so you're not rearranging the configuration in the dark. If you have a big enough tent, arrange your gear bags at the perimeter. But make sure nothing is butting up against the tent walls. Anything touching the walls can draw moisture, either dew or rain, from the outside into the tent. If space is at a premium, stow bags in the tent's vestibule.

Main Tent: The Sanctuary

Only once did we let the kids (and their friends) go nuts and play in the tent after all the bags and pads were set up. Never again, I tell you. Not only were all the sleeping bags heaped in an unruly pile (and yes, maybe I'm a touch OCD here), but the kids also tracked in so much dirt and dust that I ended up having an asthma attack in the middle of the night. So, unless you have a high tolerance for chaos and dirt, my recommendation is to declare the tent a sanctuary of peace and serenity where children and adults sleep like babies. Once the boudoir is situated, the tent is off-limits to roughhousing.

Play Tent: Thunderdome

The problem with the Tent as Sanctuary policy is that for kids, roughhousing in the tent is half the fun of camping. The solution is to bring along a small kid's play tent or the old orange pup tent from your scouting days. Let the wild things wrestle, cavort, and otherwise wreak havoc in that tent, muddy sandals and all. This way you can preserve order and tranquillity in the family tent.

The Kitchen: Triangulation

At campsites with established tent pads, fire rings, and picnic tables, your camp setup won't require much thought. But if you're at a site that's less formal, you need to figure out what will be the best arrangement.

When setting up the camp kitchen, the first thing to consider is the location of your tent. You want the kitchen to be as far from the tent as possible (within reason), because you don't want your tent smelling like blueberry cobbler. Bears love blueberry cobbler.

When laying out an efficient kitchen plan, modern kitchen designers create a work triangle between refrigerator, cooktop, and sink. Do this at camp with the cooler, the camp stove, and the washing station. You want your triangle to be near the counter space, which at a campsite is defined as the picnic table. In the absence of a picnic table, look for a flat spot that's free of grass, leaves, and other combustibles for your stove, and a flat patch or rock for food prep.

THE CAMPFIRE: LET THE FLAMES BEGIN!

The campfire is a tradition so entwined with camping that for many people, no campsite is complete without a fire ring. Memories are forged by tossing pinecones into the flames and watching sparks fly like miniature pyrotechnics. Steaks sizzle and marshmallows molt over embers burning red hot. With its warm luminescent glow, the hypnotizing dance of flickering flames, and the delightful soundtrack of cracking and hissing, the campfire is quintessential, really, to the camping experience.

For kids, learning to build a campfire is a rite of passage. You get to teach children the finer points of campfire construction, all the while channeling your own inner pyromaniac. Ahem: what I meant to say was, all the while modeling appropriate respect for this awesome force of nature. In any case, the appeal of the campfire cannot be denied.

Here's the fly in the ointment: campfires aren't so hot for the environment—or your health, for that matter. As wood burns, it releases a number of potential carcinogens, including particulate matter, which is a health risk for anyone, but especially for people with asthma or compromised lung function. In fact, a study by the Environmental Protection Agency (EPA) found that mice exposed to wood smoke were more susceptible to respiratory infection than mice exposed to fumes from an oil furnace and to regular air. After being exposed to wood smoke and then to a flu bug, 21 percent of the mice died, versus a 5 percent mortality rate among the control group.[1] You better hope the smoke clears when you chant, "I hate white rabbits."

A campfire built or extinguished without care can cause a forest fire, clearly a monumental environmental impact. And the balance of a wilderness ecosystem can be upset by hordes of campers collecting firewood every weekend. Insects, birds, and small animals make homes in snags and downed trees. Decomposing deadfall provides a forest floor with the nutrients needed for future tree growth.

Fire is a hazard not to be taken lightly, especially if your children are small. You don't want your toddler tripping headlong into the inferno. Yet the allure of fire is irresistible to most kids. Mine are forever chucking twigs and pine needles into the blaze. They also like stirring the embers with sticks—and then waving the long, red-hot pokers in the air all willy-nilly. The only thing worse than a poke in the eye with a sharp stick is a poke in the eye with a *sizzling-hot* sharp stick.

Because of the environmental pitfalls, many backcountry areas do not permit campfires, or they require permits. Increasingly, backpackers are relying on camp stoves for cooking, and lanterns and headlamps for light.

Lanterns with candles can emulate that soft, warm glow you might miss from a campfire.

When it comes to car camping, campfires are still the norm. So go ahead and enjoy a campfire. Just be sure to take steps to minimize the environmental impact and maximize the safety factor of your campfire. And remember, fires are like toddlers around deep water: never *ever* leave them unattended.

Campfire Fuel: Collect Wood before You Go

Many campgrounds have rules against collecting firewood, which means you'll need to buy stacks of split logs from the campsite host, visitor center, or ranger station. You can save a few dollars by buying wood at your local grocery store before you leave town. Unless you're crossing state lines, that is. Because firewood can harbor invasive insects, many campgrounds now have bans on out-of-state firewood. Vermont doesn't want you importing the Asian Longhorned Beetle, and Kentucky wants no part of the Emerald Ash Borer.

SMART TIP When rummaging the forest floor for firewood, follow the four Ds policy—dead, down, distant, and dinky—from the folks at the Leave No Trace Center for Outdoor Ethics, which teaches people how to enjoy the outdoors responsibly.

If collecting firewood around the campground is allowed, you should still follow certain guidelines to keep your impact low. Collect only dead, fallen timber; never cut or break branches from standing trees. Find wood that's distant from your campsite to spread the impact of your foraging. Gather wood that's shorter than the length of your forearm and smaller than the diameter of your wrist. You should be able to break the wood with your hands. At the end of your trip, you don't want to leave behind unsightly hunks of half-burned logs in the fire ring.

Where to Build a Fire

Established campgrounds nearly always have existing fire rings. Use them. Then you won't char another area of soil, move rocks, or worry about safe placement.

If you are allowed to build a fire where there is no existing fire ring, choose ground that is sandy or gravelly, rather than rich soil. Clear away any combustible organic matter, like dry grasses, sticks, and leaves. Take care not to build a fire underneath any low-hanging tree limbs—or the temporary clothesline draped with your new hiking shorts. Make sure the fire is positioned well away from your tent. You can place some big rocks in a circle to create a fire ring, but be sure to return the rocks when you are finished.

SMART TIP Do your best to control your pyromaniacal tendencies. Keeping fires small helps to conserve wood.

Stack firewood away from the fire ring. Even a log sitting just outside a fire ring can catch on fire. I've seen it happen.

How to Build a Fire

When you hear on the news that an errant cigarette butt or the charred love letter of a jilted forest-service worker started a raging forest fire, you might think that fires start easily. And they certainly can, given the right conditions. But on occasion, say a damp soggy day, you can have the dickens of a time getting a campfire going. You could ask my husband about this.

Knowing how to build a campfire is not only a good way to impress your kids but is also critical know-how for wilderness survival. If you were ever lost in the woods, a fire could save your bacon. The first thing is to know your types of fuel. Tinder is something small and highly flammable, such as

FLAME TIME: BUILD A ROARING CAMPFIRE, STEP-BY-STEP

① ② ③ ④ ⑤ ⑥ matches ⑦ ⑧

See instructions on how to build
a fire on pages 73–74.

twigs, dry grasses, pine needles, crumpled newspaper or notepaper, dryer lint, wood shavings, dry leaves. Kindling is made up of slightly bigger sticks and twigs, from pencil to finger diameter. Next are wrist-width sticks and finally logs, which are bigger yet and longer burning.

The brain trust at Leave No Trace suggests putting nothing wider around than your wrist into a backcountry fire. If you're car camping, you likely bought a bundle of split logs, which are more the size of a toddler's thigh, but you didn't collect them around the campground, so it's okay.

Tinder sparks up the kindling; small kindling ignites bigger kindling; kindling fires up big sticks; big sticks light the logs. Simple, no? Follow these basic instructions to get a campfire roaring.

1. Before you strike a match, collect your tinder, kindling, and sticks. If you brought or bought split logs, have them stacked nearby. You can't feed a fire if you're out in the woods looking for deadfall.

2. Arrange your wood collection in size order, so you can quickly grab the right size of fuel as you stoke the fire.

3. Have a large container or bucket of water on hand in case the flames and sparks get too wild, and you need to douse the fire quickly.

4. In the center of your fire pit, place three half-inch-wide sticks to create a small triangular platform for the tinder. Pack a bunch of tinder (tiny twigs, pine needles, dry grasses) about the size of a softball on top of the triangle. The platform allows you to light the tinder from below.

5. Next, build a teepee of kindling (starting with the pencil-width sticks) over the tinder, leaving a gap in case you need to stuff in more tinder. The teepee design creates small chimneys that will move flames through the fuel. Don't pack on too much kindling at first; you need a design that's loose enough to allow for air circulation. Fire needs oxygen to burn.

6. Using your ignition tool of choice, light the tinder. Use matches, a butane lighter, a small steel and flint, or a magnesium spark-making device. If the burgeoning fire needs coaxing, gently blow on the tinder to get it going.

7. Once the smaller kindling catches, start adding the finger-width kindling to the teepee. Keep adding increasingly bigger sticks until you're adding wrist-diameter sticks and logs.

8. If the fire wanes at any time in the process, you can use a plastic or paper plate to fan the flames.

Cooking Fire-Licked Food

For more info on cooking over a campfire, see "Cooking Modes: Stoves, Campfires, and Charcoal Grills," page 90.

Never Burn Trash: Pack It Out

Burning wood alone sends particulate matter skyward. Add cans, plastic bags or bottles, Styrofoam, or foil, and the fire will release toxic fumes containing carcinogens like dioxins, benzene, styrene, furan, lead, and mercury. Even chip bags, candy wrappers, and coated cardboard can release harmful chemicals when burned. This is bad. Newspaper and uncoated cardboard are okay to burn, but your best bet is to stick with wood and pack out your trash.

CAMPFIRE CHECKLIST

- ☐ Homemade or store-bought fire-starting tinder
- ☐ Tinder collected at the campsite
- ☐ Kindling
- ☐ Larger sticks
- ☐ Bundle of firewood
- ☐ Matches, lighter, or fire starter
- ☐ Paper or plastic plate

Extinguishing a Campfire

When you've finished enjoying your campfire—before you turn in for the night, before leaving the campsite in the morning, and before you pack up and head home—it's critical that you put out the fire properly.

First, let the wood burn down to ash. At this point, it may look like the fire is out, but hot embers lurking

SECRET WEAPON: HOMEMADE FIRE-STARTING EGGS

You can't just flick a Bic to a log and start a blaze. You have to start small and grow the fire. Tinder is your starting point, but sometimes, especially on rainy days, the tinder you collect around the campsite is damp and defies flame.

A good backup plan is to bring along commercially made emergency tinder. Coghlan's has one that looks like a cotton plug soaked in wax. Lightning Nuggets makes balls of compressed, pulverized pitch wood that will burn for up to fifteen minutes, plenty long enough to get the kindling going. And Ultimate Survival has a fire-starting tinder cube that will light even when floating in water.

You can also make your own fire-starting tinder at home. The easiest way to create homemade emergency tinder is to slather cotton balls in petroleum jelly. Store them in a zip-top baggie or an old pill container.

A more involved but fun project to do with the kids is to make fire starters in cardboard egg cartons. (This is where Martha Stewart and Bear Grylls meet back on the other side.) Because you are using recycled materials like dryer lint, sawdust, and candle stubs, this is truly a green craft. Taking care when melting the wax is critical—unless you're looking to burn down the kitchen and collect the insurance money. Wax vapor is extremely flammable, which is why these fire starters are so effective. One fire-starting egg will burn for upwards of five minutes. Melt the wax over an electric heat source rather than the open flame of a gas stove. Use a double-boiler setup so the wax isn't in direct contact with the heat source.

MATERIALS

• Cardboard egg carton
• Sawdust or dryer lint
• Unscented candle stubs (or paraffin)

- Large aluminum can
- Pot for boiling water
- Electric heat source
- Pot lifters or pliers
- Metal cookie cutters (optional)

INSTRUCTIONS

1. Stuff the twelve sections of a cardboard egg carton with sawdust or dryer lint, or a combination of the two.
2. Clean out an old fifteen-ounce can (from stewed tomatoes, refried beans, or the like). Squeeze the can and crimp one side so you can pour the wax easily.
3. Put a handful of candle stubs in the can.
4. Fill a big pot with two inches of water. Create a double boiler by placing the can of wax into the water. If you have so much wax that it sinks to the bottom of the pot, set metal cookie cutters underneath the can to keep it elevated.
5. Boil the water and watch the wax carefully. As soon as it melts (about twenty minutes), use your camping pot lifters or pliers to pick up the can. Slowly pour a layer of the melted wax on top of each of the tinder-filled egg carton reservoirs.
6. Once the wax cools, use a serrated knife to saw the egg carton into twelve fire-starting balls.
7. In camp, set a fire-starting egg into the middle of your kindling teepee and light the cardboard edge.

in the ash pile are enough to ignite a forest fire, given the right gust. Pour water on the remains of the fire and keep the water coming until you no longer

SMART TIP

Collect dryer lint to use as tinder. It's essentially made up of tiny bits of cotton, and as such, it's highly flammable.

hear hissing noises. Stir the wet-ash mixture with a stick. Add more water. You're good to go when the ash mixture is cold to the touch. Water is preferable to dirt for extinguishing a fire, but if you don't have water, dirt is the next best thing.

If you're at a campground, the camp hosts will likely clean out the ash for incoming campers. But if you're in the backcountry, you should either bury your ashes or scatter them over a large area. On some rivers, you may be required to pack out ashes.

CAMPSITE ETIQUETTE

Campsite etiquette may sound a tad oxymoronic. Do you really need to mind your manners when you're rolling around in the dirt? The short answer is yes. Campsite etiquette isn't so much about properly identifying the fish fork and keeping your elbows off the table. It's about being kind to the environment and considerate of your camping neighbors.

There is no better time than a camping trip to encourage children to become stewards of the land. Being out in the woods, surrounded by the scent of pine and the plaintive cries of a loon, can instill a wonder in kids that will stay with them the rest of their lives. Foster a respect for nature in your children now, and they'll be more inclined to help preserve the environment for future generations.

Not so long ago in Yellowstone, it was common practice to make a wish and toss spare change into pools and geysers. More egregious yet, some visitors simply hurled trash into the hydrothermal springs. One erstwhile geyser, now called Morning Glory Pool, no longer erupts because it's clogged with litter. This iridescent azure and turquoise pool is the inspiration for a lovely children's book by Jan Brett called *Hedgie Blasts Off!* In the story, a hedgehog is dispatched into space to unplug Big Sparkler, a space geyser that has become plugged up over time by aliens hurling coins into it. Talk about a teachable one-two punch. The combination of reading the book countless nights and seeing the inspirational pool in real time has left a lasting impression on our kids. They have become pint-sized preservationists.

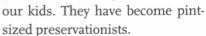

Carry a small plastic bag for your own garbage and for any litter you pick up along the trail.

Don't Leave Your Mark

Camping affords you the perfect opportunity to teach kids about reducing our impact on the environment. On any given hike, chances are you'll see evidence of previous generations who clearly did not embrace the "tread lightly" ethic. You'll see scars on trees where people have carved their names into the bark—"Dwayne loves Brandy"—professing love in a way that's very unloving to trees. My kids see those scars and shout, "A bonehead did that!" (I'm not saying they heard that from me.)

This is the time to talk to kids about phloem and xylem, and how carving deep into the bark of a tree is not unlike cutting through our skin and gouging veins and arteries. Even shallow scratches in a tree can leave it vulnerable to damaging insects and disease. Teach kids to understand and appreciate trees as living things, and maybe they won't waste so much toilet paper.

Coach children to stay on the trail and walk single file to reduce erosion and support plant growth. Hiking with kids nearly always means lots of trailside breaks. If you pull off to the side of a trail, try to rest your butts on a durable surface like a rock or a fallen log rather than on a patch of delicate wildflowers or fragile alpine tundra. When you're finished with a trailside snack, make sure to clean up any food bits and pick up any wrappers. Dole out bonus points for picking up garbage others have left on the trail. You'll need to help kids determine what's safe to pick up. Our kids are so conditioned to pick up trash on the trail that they have come to us with proud smiles and chunks of broken glass.

Resources for Responsible Recreation

A valuable resource for eco-conscious campers is Tread Lightly!, an organization dedicated to responsible outdoor recreation. Their website features a kids' section with games, a quiz, a downloadable coloring book, and a Tread Pledge filled with tips for treading lightly (www.treadlightly.org).

Leave No Trace, an organization with a similar mission, offers an educational program designed to teach outdoor enthusiasts to minimize their impact on the environment. Find a complete and detailed list of Leave No Trace principles, as well as information on programs and events in your area, at www.lnt.org.

No Poaching

The vision of a toddler collecting a bouquet of wildflowers is sweet, but it must be discouraged. You want to leave the flowers for others to enjoy. Many people wonder what the harm is in plucking a daisy from a meadow full of wildflowers. And they're right. One daisy is no big deal. But if every hiker on a busy trail picked a big old bunch, there would be few flowers left. For an exception to this rule, see "Pressed Flowers," page 175.

Similarly, when your child starts collecting cool rocks, you should repeat the environmentalist's mantra: take only pictures, leave only footprints. You don't want five pounds of rocks in your car anyway. Leaving the wilderness as you found it is a good all-around policy, but it's especially important in national parks, where it's illegal to remove any natural object.

Of course, kids just love collecting things. While we're camping, we let them collect pinecones, rocks, feathers, and sticks. But before we head home, the booty gets dispersed in the woods around the campsite.

Be a Tidy Camper

It's important to keep your campsite clear of food and garbage. Even during the day when you're off on a hike, keep all food locked in the trunk of the car or in a bear box. Regularly empty your trash into the campground's animal-proof dumpster. You don't want to attract wildlife to your campsite. For more on keeping your campsite critter-free, see "Camp Kitchen Cleanup," page 111. And tempting as it may be, discourage kids from feeding crumbs to little creatures like chipmunks and birds. Read more about the negative impact of feeding wildlife in "Wildlife Watching," page 132.

Always do a thorough cleanup of your campsite before you leave. This includes cleaning up after a campfire. See page 74 for more on campfires, and page 83 for tips on breaking down camp.

Quiet Hours

Most campgrounds have set quiet hours, usually from 10 P.M. until 7 A.M. Those restrictions are a good thing, especially for families. The success of a camping trip can hinge on the quality and quantity of sleep your kids get. There's nothing worse than finally settling down a child who had been brimming with excitement about sleeping outside, only to have them woken up by a loud talker passing by the campsite.

At 6 A.M., your job is to keep any early wakers quiet while the loud talker is still sleeping. And yes, you'll be taking the higher ground by not exacting revenge on said loud talker.

Keep the Hellions under Control

Respect your fellow campers (especially the elderly couple next door) by keeping track of your little rascals and teaching them to respect boundaries. The bane of car camping compared with backpacking is the loss of privacy and solitude. Often you'll be camping cheek by jowl with perfect strangers. Nobody wants a bunch of screaming six-year-olds running through their campsite.

Shortly after I'd finished reading Richard Louv's *Last Child in the Woods*, we took a camping trip to Black Canyon of the Gunnison National Park. Inspired by Louv's treatise, my husband and I made an intentional decision to let the kids run loose. We wanted to give them the freedom to explore and to commune with nature. To let their imaginations run free in the wild and replenish the nature deficit Louv cautions against.

The problem with the long-leash program was twofold: First, we realized the route to their new secret fort ran right through the backyards of three campsites. Second, the next day we spotted a young bear cub ambling around the campground. Gulp. Better to tighten the leash enough to keep kids safe and respectful of others.

Lighten Up the Lead Foot

Car-camping campgrounds usually have speed limits in the neighborhood of fifteen miles per hour. The snail's pace is for good reason. When kids are riding bikes and darting across the road to chase lizards, it's bad form to drive like Mario Andretti.

A Word on the Playing of Loud Music

We take our children camping to immerse ourselves in nature and unplug from the electronic, battery-operated world we live in. It's not that we crave silence, because the woods after dark can be downright cacophonous. There's the crackle, pop, and hiss of the campfire. The roar of a river gushing past. Owls hoot, crickets chirp. The shrill whir of the cicada can reach a hundred decibels, higher than the legal noise-ordinance level of some cities. Still, we do not go camping to be assaulted by Lil Wayne or Def Leppard thumping from a boom box.

At most car-camping locations, the sites are often clustered together. You are just a few feet, really, from the next site, yet you are not buffered from your neighbors by layers of stucco, brick, insulation, and wallboard. Sound travels effortlessly through millimeter-thick tent walls: you can hear fellow campers snoring and babies crying at the site next door.

At the risk of sounding curmudgeonly, for the love of Sam Hill, leave the iPod and portable speakers at home. If your kids are tweens or teens, and

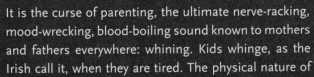

FIVE WAYS TO CURB WHINING

It is the curse of parenting, the ultimate nerve-racking, mood-wrecking, blood-boiling sound known to mothers and fathers everywhere: whining. Kids whinge, as the Irish call it, when they are tired. The physical nature of camping—all the climbing on rocks and swinging from vines—guarantees that your kids will be dog tired. Although tired is good, whining is bad. We can all agree on this. On your next camp outing, try these tactics to mitigate the whining.

1. *Lower your expectations.* As parents, we all endure a fair amount of whining because we pack too much into our day. We want to do it all, see it all. Admittedly, I'm one of those people who feel compelled to make it to the top of every last peak. Now that I have kids, I've learned to get over my summit fever. It's okay if it takes all morning to get a half mile down a trail. It's okay to just hang around at the campsite and let the kids play with pinecones. If we're in a national park, maybe we don't need to see every landmark and stop at every last overlook. As long as your children are outside and having fun in nature, you can consider your camping trip a success.

2. *Stay focused on the kids.* Often, our kids start to whinge when my husband and I are wrapped up in a conversation and we are essentially ignoring them. When we interact with the kids on the trail or at the campsite, they stay engaged and happy.

3. *Distract them.* If you have a good memory for jokes and riddles, you can throw one out whenever little campers get ornery. If your memory is more like mine—which is to say, more like a sieve than a sponge—bring along a small joke or riddle book. Ridiculous knock-knock jokes can deflect a child's attention on hikes, during long car rides, and while waiting for dinner. And kids will soon forget what they were whining about when

they're trying to figure out how to get the fox, the chicken, and the head of cabbage across the river.

4. *Feed the beasts.* My brother Gerard, who is pushing fifty, turns into a five-year-old when he isn't properly fed. I'm telling you, the guy gets crabby. So just imagine what happens when you don't feed a five-year-old. There's nothing that fuels whining like an empty stomach. Best to never let it happen while camping. In addition to three solid square meals, be armed with granola bars, fruit, cheese sticks, and other nibblies at all times.

5. *Use earplugs.* I am not kidding about this. If all else fails and all basic needs have been fulfilled and the kids are still using that most irritating of tones, it's best to simply muffle it. Whining is easier to ignore when you can't really hear it. This tactic is best employed in the car when there is nothing much you can do about it anyway. Keep a pair of earplugs in the glove compartment. And so you can feel good about your seeming inattentiveness, know that parenting experts call this "purposeful ignoring."

you can't pry the iPods from their clenched fists, at least bring headphones. Hopefully, you can convince them to pop out the earbuds for just a little while and instead tune in to the frequency of the night air.

BREAKING DOWN CAMP

The good news about breaking down camp versus gearing up for a camping trip is that the job is finite. Packing up can literally take days. And you're never quite sure when you've got it all done. There could be something critical buried in the garage that you haven't packed yet. When the task is simply a matter of getting everything from the campsite back into the car, it's a fixed job with a predictable end in sight.

As you did with the camp setup, try to make the chore of breaking down camp a fun part of the overall camping adventure. Enlist kids to help roll up sleeping pads and stuff sleeping bags into sacks. Have them help dismantle the tent and tote pillows and small bags to the car.

The Tent: Deconstruction Time

Tents are a little like paper road maps: they're easy to open up, but you can never get them folded back up the same way. In the case of tents, that means neatly zipped up in the storage bag the way it arrived from the factory.

When deconstructing collapsible tent poles with shock cords, start pulling them apart at the middle rather than at one end. This way the cord has equal tension throughout while in storage.

If possible, wait until the morning sun has completely dried off any rain or dew from your tent. If you pack a tent while it's wet, you'll need to erect it in the backyard or hang it on a line to dry out when you get home. Otherwise you're asking for mold and mildew. If you're camping in wet conditions, you may not have a choice. You'll need to dry the tent at home.

Because tents (and their storage bags) come in all shapes and sizes, there's no single right way to fold up a tent. Some campers just stuff the tent back in the bag the way they stuff a sleeping bag in a sack. And that works, too. But generally speaking, once you've removed all the stakes and poles, you want to fold the tent lengthwise with the door at one end—in halves, thirds, or quarters, depending on the size of the poles and storage bag. The key is to keep the door unzipped to prevent air bubbles.

Give the folded tent a little shake or wipe the underside with a rag to remove the better part of the dirt. Neatly fold the rainfly so it's the same width as the tent and place it on top. Next, set your collapsed tent poles at the end *opposite* the door. Have kids roll the tent tightly around the poles all the way to the door end. As they squeeze and roll the tent, the trapped air will escape out the door. Then you can stuff the whole enchilada into the tent bag.

At home, store your tent in a cool, dry place. Tent makers recommend that you store your tent loosely in a larger nonplastic bag or box, rather than compressed in its original stuff sack. They also advise that you store tent poles assembled so the shock cords don't wear out. This is all well and good if you have an empty barn or a spacious four-car garage at your disposal. But storing tent and poles separately is a recipe for disaster, if you ask me. I'd rather have to replace my shock cords periodically than arrive at a campground without tent poles. You cannot make do without tent poles. It's your call on whether or not to heed that particular nugget of advice.

SMART TIP When it's time to break camp, instead of using a dustpan and broom to sweep the dirt and pine needles that have inevitably found their way into the tent, simply remove the rainfly, unstake the tent, lift the tent overhead (poles still in place and doors zipped open), and shake. It may take two people to hoist the tent, but the dust will spill right out the door.

Sleeping Bags: Neatness Doesn't Count

For backpacking and for economy of space when car camping, you'll want to compress sleeping bags into their stuff sacks. But forget rolling them up neatly like little Ho Hos. The best practice is to grab the foot end of the bag and cram it into the stuff sack. And keep grabbing sections of bag and jamming them in until it's all in there and your biceps are burning.

When you get home from a trip, pull the sleeping bags out of the stuff sacks, turn them inside out, and air them out for a few days. Store sleeping bags in large cotton bags. If one didn't come with your bag, you can get them separately at camp stores and from sleeping-bag manufacturers. Storing a sleeping bag tightly in its compression stuff sack can, over time, reduce a sleeping bag's loft. You don't want to crush all those precious goose feathers.

Campsite Cleanup: Neatness Counts

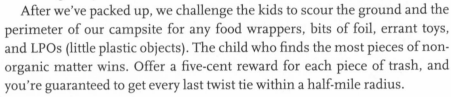

Your goal at departure time should be to leave the campsite cleaner than you found it. Getting your trash in the Dumpster is a given, but many campgrounds now have recycling bins for cans and bottles. If not, pack them in the car and recycle them at home. Consider double bagging the recycling so you don't have a slimy mixture of stale beer and flat Coke dripping on your new Patagonia jacket.

After we've packed up, we challenge the kids to scour the ground and the perimeter of our campsite for any food wrappers, bits of foil, errant toys, and LPOs (little plastic objects). The child who finds the most pieces of non-organic matter wins. Offer a five-cent reward for each piece of trash, and you're guaranteed to get every last twist tie within a half-mile radius.

Chapter Four

CAMP GRUB

Snoopy thought the birds would pack food, tents, and compasses. He rolled his eyes when he saw Woodstock return with golf clubs, and Harriet carefully holding her angel food cake with seven-minute frosting. Snoopy wondered if the birds understood camping in the wilderness.

—*Take a Hike, Snoopy!* by Judy Katschke

Sitting atop Colorado's Mount Democrat, a 14,155-foot peak in the Mosquito Range, surrounded by a rumple of jagged peaks scraping a blue-bird sky, I had an epiphany. As I munched on summer sausage and extra-sharp cheddar on a delightfully crisp whole-grain cracker, it occurred to me that the best thing about reaching the top of a mountain was *eating* on top of a mountain. Really. Food just tastes better when you are up high on a peak or deep in the woods.

When you're camping, food transcends survival: it can actually define your camping experience. For epicures, the challenge of conjuring sublime camp food is half the fun. There is a certain triumph in going gourmet miles from a kitchen. For others, a couple of dogs on the end of a stick will do. It all tastes good when you're camping. The best PB&J on Wonder Bread I ever had was on a winter hike with my brothers when I was ten. I remember it to this day.

PLAN THE MENU WELL SO YOU CAN HAVE YOUR GORP AND EAT IT, TOO

PEANUT BUTTER

CAMP GRUB

① Dinner
② Breakfast
③ Lunch
④ Dessert
⑤ Snacks
⑥ Liquids

See suggested camp recipes on pages 94–110.

TRAIL BAR

Milk 1%

Whether you go gourmet or basic, you need to think the menu through. Otherwise you'll be straining spaghetti through your bandana. Below are tactics for successful camp mealtimes, including information on planning, packing, and prepping. In this section, you'll also find a weekend's worth of camp recipes and tips for successful camp cleanup. Try to stay flexible, though, because you will undoubtedly forget something. We once completely overlooked breakfast for the last morning of a backpacking trip. We ended up frying a mash of leftover steak and potatoes. The kids griped at first, but it was one of the heartiest and tastiest breakfasts we've ever had.

PLANNING, PACKING, AND PREPPING CAMP MEALS

Start by writing out daily menus for the trip—breakfast, lunch, snacks, dinner, and dessert. Run through the menu and make a note of the condiments and spices you'll need for each meal. Salt and pepper, ketchup, mayo, mustard, Cholula Hot Sauce. If your kids are like mine, they will freak out if you forget the ketchup.

Next, create a shopping list based on the menu. When it comes time to pack the cookware, visualize what you'll need to prepare each dish and to eat it. Make cookware notes on the menu: a spatula for fried eggs, bowls for stew, a frying pan for bacon.

Now here's the critical piece: before you roll out of the driveway, run through your annotated menu and check items off as you go, making sure you've got everything you need. Don't forget any items you might have in the freezer.

Consider making your life easier by eating the first meal of your trip at a restaurant (or grabbing sandwiches from a sub shop), especially if it's your first time family camping. This may prove particularly wise if you are getting to your campsite on a Friday night. Setting up camp will be more manageable if everyone is operating on a full stomach. Similarly, at the tail end of a trip, it might be best to pack up, beat a hasty retreat, and grab your final breakfast at a diner on the way back home. You won't lose any points with the camping police for taking these shortcuts. When you're traveling with kids, you have to go with the Whatever Works approach.

Cooking Modes: Stoves, Campfires, and Charcoal Grills

When planning a camp menu, you need to chart out the heat source for each meal. You can do most of your cooking over a camp stove, which is the environmentally correct way to go. But there are certain menu items that you may opt to grill over an open flame. Steaks, beer brats, and hot dogs come to mind. Many campground fire pits have cooking grates, which swing out of the way when not in use and swing over the coals when you're ready to grill.

In the absence of a permanent grate, you'll need to bring your own. On backpacking trips, we've propped a simple baker's cooling rack across the stones of a fire ring. This setup works just fine, albeit a little wobbly. At camp stores you can find simple, collapsible steel grids with legs, which are designed to stand over a campfire.

Remember to plan ahead if you want to cook over the fire. You'll need to start the fire, stoke it, then let it burn down to coals before you start cooking. The camp stove, which you can light in a matter of seconds, is a good backstop if you find yourself in the predinner witching hour and the fire isn't even started yet.

A third option at many established campgrounds is to grill over charcoal. Call ahead or check online to see if the campground has charcoal grills. If you plan to use these grills, remember to pack a bag of briquettes and lighter fluid.

Packing Food: Light and Tight

Even if you're car camping, it's best to pack your camp pantry efficiently. It makes the load lighter and makes it easier to find things when you're in the field. Take a cue from my mother: nothing in her kitchen is still in its original packaging. She shops at Costco and then repackages and portions everything into smaller containers. Milk is in Gatorade bottles, and jelly beans are in jam jars. If you pull a tin can of biscotti out of her pantry, you are more likely to find tea bags.

Pack condiments in small Tupperware containers. You just don't need that industrial-sized bottle of mustard. Remove any unnecessary plastic and cardboard packaging from food. Whether it's granola bars, cookies, or Goldfish, portion out what you think the kids will eat on the trip and put it in sealable plastic bags. Glass is nice to store food in at home, but use plastic containers for camping. They're lightweight and won't shatter.

Run through each meal's recipe, and do whatever pre-prep you can at home. Chop up vegetables. Measure and mix the dry ingredients for pancakes. Pour salt and pepper into miniature shakers (available at camp stores). If a recipe calls for spices, measure them out and transport them in small plastic bags. Make sure to label spices and what dish they're destined for so you don't mix up the cayenne with the cinnamon. Or worse yet, the oregano with the medical marijuana.

Camp Pantry: Organizing the Dry Goods

At home, I know where everything is stored in my kitchen pantry. The cereal boxes are always on the top shelf to the right of the refrigerator, and

Remember to print out and bring along recipes. Or, if you've pre-prepped a meal, use a permanent marker to write the remainder of the instructions right on the plastic freezer bag that you stored the food in.

my emergency stash of good dark chocolate is secreted behind the tea bags. When you're camping, you need to have a similar game plan so you can reach in a bag and pull out the burger buns without major rooting around.

One tactic is to stow the dry goods by meal in separate canvas bags. Pack all the breakfast foods in one bag and label it with a permanent marker on a piece of masking tape. Repeat for snacks, lunch, and dinner foods.

Another way to organize food is a base-camp storage system like Kelty's Binto Bar. Three rectangular bags slide into a big fabric box, and each bag has a clever plastic window where you can slip in a bit of paper with a detailed list of the bag's contents. When it's time to look for that tiny container of gummi bears, you know which bag to dig in.

Camp Cooler: Packing the Perishables

For a weekend camping trip, the ice in a food cooler should last. But if the weather is scorching, you may need to search out the closest grocery or campground store to add ice each day. If that's not possible, you need to plan and eat tactically. Eat the food that's most perishable on the first night. Steaks, chicken, burgers. The arugula and cucumber salad. Peaches and raspberries.

SMART TIP Make a hearty stew or soup ahead of time and freeze it. The hunk of frozen dinner will help keep the cooler cold and will defrost in time for the second or third night's dinner.

Save foods that last longer for later in the trip. Dry foods like pasta, rice, noodles, cereal, and energy bars will last longer than you will. Thanks to preservatives, cold cuts will keep the weekend in a cooler, and bacon, salami, and hot dogs will keep even longer. Kept cool, eggs will be fine for days. Chunks of hard cheese like sharp cheddar, Parmesan, and aged Gouda can last a week easily. Apples and oranges will stand up, even outside the cooler, as long as they're not cut up.

If you're backpacking, food planning is a whole different can of beans. With no cooler, your best bets are dried foods like jerky, pasta, dehydrated fruit, and freeze-dried meals that you reconstitute with water.

Resist the Temptation to Overpack

When you're packing the food cooler, don't panic. The pitfall here is to fear starvation in the woods. That's when you start emptying your fridge and chucking everything into the cooler. We invariably bring too much food, and by the time we drive home, what's left in the cooler is pretty nasty.

To avoid wasteful leftovers, think portion control. How many oatmeal packets will each person eat at breakfast? How much rib eye will the kids really eat? Grab only a handful of pasta for each adult, less for kids. Cut the enormous chunk of Parmesan in half. Pour milk and juice from the gallon jugs into smaller plastic bottles.

SMART TIP To keep the pileup of glass bottles and aluminum cans to a minimum, bring along powdered drink mixes. Choose a powdered sports drink like Gatorade over ultrasweet drinks like Kool-Aid. Sports drinks have considerably less sugar and help replace electrolytes lost on a sweaty slog up a mountain.

Drinks: Happy Hour

Throughout the day, we ply our kids with water to keep them hydrated. But at the end of a long day of hiking and otherwise playing hard in the woods, there's nothing like a fancy bottle of handcrafted root beer. We allot one bottle per kid, per day, and keep it chilling in the cooler until happy hour. To keep our kids moving down the trail, we dangle the soda like a carrot on a stick. Root beers, we say, are for hard-core hikers.

In the backcountry, you'd be unwise to tote six packs of Bud longnecks. You're better with a plastic flask of single malt. Or maybe a little peppermint schnapps to spike your cocoa. It's also a treat to sip a bodacious pinot noir with your freeze-dried lasagna when you're miles from the trailhead. A company called Platypus makes collapsible plastic bladders for carrying and preserving wine in the backcountry.

For car camping, consider bringing boxed wine (also called BIB, for Bag-in-Box) or wine sold simply in an airtight plastic bladder with a built-in spigot. Before you turn your nose up, know that in Europe, oenophiles have been drinking premium wines in boxes for some time now. Screw-top wine bottles once had a bad name, too. Eliminating all those green glass bottles is environmentally conscious, the wine lasts longer because the bladder-and-spigot system protects it from oxygen, and a box of chilled white will stay cold for a good long time. And it's way more economical than buying bottles.

The beauty of car camping is that you can have a dedicated drink cooler. If you're a beer snob—excuse me, *connoisseur*—like me, you'll be glad to know that more and more brewers are crafting tasty beers in cans. Oskar Blues of Lyons, Colorado, makes half a dozen hand-canned beers, but the most appropriate canned beer for the campsite has to be an India Pale Ale from the Santa Fe Brewing Company called Happy Camper.

If you can't live without a frozen margarita, bring along a hand-cranked blender that clamps onto a picnic table. This gadget from GSI Outdoors proves that anything goes with car camping.

CAMP RECIPES

I hesitate to overstress the monumental importance of the camp dinner, but I swear my engagement to my husband was nearly called off over a back-woods meal gone awry. We were backpacking in the Adirondacks, and our grand plan was to summit Mount Marcy, New York's highest peak. The weekend prior, Jeff had fallen to one knee and popped the question over a gourmet picnic in the woods of New Jersey.

SMART TIP If scrambled eggs are on the menu, crack the eggs at home and pour them (with the milk and the salt and pepper) into a widemouthed Nalgene water bottle. That way, you don't need to worry about eggs cracking or egg cartons getting soggy in the cooler. At camp, just pull the bottle from your cooler, give it a shake, and dump it into the frying pan. (Be sure to cook the eggs within two days of cracking them.)

Our first mistake as a newly engaged couple was to completely botch the mileage calculations for a loop hike. On the first day, it had taken us only a few hours to cover the four miles to our campsite. But that terrain was *flat*. The next day, we charted out an eight-mile loop, but we neglected to figure in the considerable elevation gain and loss of climbing the peak. By the time we made it back to camp, it was dark and we were both exhausted. That's when I pulled out dinner: a one-pound bag of dried black beans.

Jeff, who knows a little something about cooking, looked absolutely murderous. "You know you need to soak these *overnight*?" I did not know that. We simmered the beans for several hours over our tiny stove. Eventually, we just gave in and ate the beans. They were exceedingly crunchy and gritty.

PS: The day Jeff proposed, I got bitten by one of those pestiferous New Jersey ticks and subsequently contracted Lyme disease. I am happy to report that thus far I've survived both the Lyme and the marriage.

Following are a weekend's worth of recipes and ideas. No black beans, I promise. Over time, these have become our family's go-to camp fare. The first night, we usually grill New York strip steaks and burgers, and serve them with corn on the cob. (Just soak the corn in the husks in salted water for an hour, wrap them in foil, and toss the ears right in the fire for fifteen to twenty minutes.)

With a little ingenuity, you can make almost anything in the woods. Of course, the more camp cookware you have at your disposal, the more variety you can have in your menu. If you simply must have warm apple-cinnamon popovers, then you might consider buying a camp oven. (See "Cookware," page 38.) But it's certainly not necessary to load up on cooking gadgets. We've made plenty of delicious meals on an old two-burner Coleman stove.

My golden rule of camp menu planning with kids is to do a dry run with any new dish at home. Introduce coq au vin in the field, and I'm telling you, your precious darlings will pronounce it "yucky." If you have no backup (because I told you not to overpack the food cooler), the kids are going to become crotchety in short order.

CAMP GRUB

Breakfast

OATMEAL WITH GOODIES

Ingredients

- Packets of instant oatmeal
- Fresh berries
- Dried fruit (cherries, apricots, raisins, cranberries)
- Sunflower seeds
- Chopped nuts (almonds, pecans, walnuts)
- Honey, maple syrup, or brown sugar

Directions

1. Dump oatmeal into bowls and add hot water according to packet directions.
2. Add the goodies.
3. Most instant packets already have copious amounts of sugar, but there are a few with just plain oats. If so, add a little honey, maple syrup, or brown sugar.

BLUEBERRY PANCAKES AND SAUSAGES (SERVES 4)

Ingredients

- 1½ cups flour
- ½ teaspoon salt
- 2½ tablespoons sugar
- 1¾ teaspoons baking powder
- 2 eggs
- 3 tablespoons melted butter
- 1¼ cup almond milk or cow's milk
- ¾ cup blueberries
- Breakfast sausages

Directions

1. At home, sift the flour twice. Mix the dry ingredients together in a large freezer bag and use a permanent marker to write the rest of the recipe on the bag.

2. At home, crack the eggs into a widemouthed Nalgene bottle and mix with the milk.*

3. In camp, whisk the wet ingredients. Add to the dry ingredients and mix lightly.

4. Melt the butter and let it cool. Fold the melted butter and then the blueberries into the pancake batter. If the batter seems too thick, add more milk.

5. Add a little butter to the pan. When the foam subsides, pour a half cup of batter for each pancake. When bubbles begin to form and bottoms are browned, flip the cakes. (About 2½ to 3 minutes.)

6. If your pan is large, you may need to rotate it around the smallish flame of the camp stove to evenly brown the pancakes.

7. In a separate pan, fry up the sausages. If there isn't enough room on your stove, you can always do the sausages first and keep them warm in a bit of foil while you make the pancakes.

* Once the eggs are cracked, be sure to cook them within two days' time.

BREWING THE PERFECT CUP OF CAMP JOE

A wispy curl of steam rises off the shimmering obsidian surface. The sweet aroma wafts through the air, rousing sleepy campers. For some, that first cup of hot coffee is nothing short of bliss. I have a friend who, as soon as she drains the dregs of her morning joe, begins to fantasize anew about rising the next day just so she can have another First Cup.

Obsession? Maybe so. For others, it's more mechanical: they just can't function without that dose of caffeine. Let's face it, a good jolt of java can really take the edge off when you're camping with kids.

There are myriad devices and techniques for brewing coffee at the campground. You can percolate, drip, or press. You can buy a fancy mechanical gas-powered device or a simple plastic filter. Regardless, it's going to taste good. On a backpacking trip near Silverton, Colorado, with our three kids (and five llamas), I had one of the most fabulous cups of coffee in memory. I had, at the last minute, tossed in a plastic jar of Folgers instant coffee nuggets that had been collecting dust in the garage since 1990. Sipped while sitting on a fallen log in a dew-covered forest, the air crisp and clear, that extra-strong, freeze-dried brew was divine.

If you're camping with other families, consider a big coffeemaker. Primus has an eight-cup coffeemaker that looks like the one on your countertop but is powered by propane. It'll keep the pot hot while you scramble your eggs. GSI Outdoors makes a six-cup, stainless-steel percolator that heats up on the camp stove.

Many companies make single coffee mugs with built-in French presses. REI has a commuter-style, stainless-steel mug with a mesh covering over the sip hole to keep out any grounds. If you're making coffee for two, Brunton makes a spiffy Flip N' Drip device. You pour boiling water into a carafe at one end, then flip it over, and coffee drips into the mug attached at the other end.

If you're backcountry camping, you don't have to go the instant-coffee route like I did. You can find plenty of nonbreakable plastic or stainless-steel French press devices or collapsible, plastic cone filters that are lightweight enough to toss in a pack. You can also find tiny espresso makers for brewing over a backcountry stove. However, using one is a balancing act involving open flame, hot fluid, and scalding steam. The first couple of times I made an espresso while camping, it ended badly. As the espresso funneled from the device into the tiny enamel espresso cup, the weight shift caused the whole contraption to tip over, the precious liquid spilling into the dirt. Once you get the hang of it, it's quite something to hear the gurgling whir of espresso spurting from a spout miles from a Starbucks.

If your purse strings are loose and your pockets deep, and you must start your day with an espresso, you can find a portable espresso machine at Illy.

Called the Handpresso, it looks like a sleek, black submachine gun out of a James Bond movie. You load it with a packet of grounds, hand-pump the shaft, add hot water, and press a button for espresso.

It would probably chap Davy Crockett's hide, but it's even possible to make a latte in the backcountry. (A double half-caf skinny macchiato, perhaps?) Snow Peak has a titanium coffee press and milk foamer that weighs in at less than a pound. Or, make a latte with a battery-operated milk frother—the kind that looks like an electric toothbrush with a tiny spinning whisk at the end. BonJour, Bodum, Ikea, and Aerolatte make frothers.

If all this sounds like too much work to get your caffeine fix, you can always just chew on a handful of chocolate-covered coffee beans and wash it back with a Red Bull.

Lunch

MOVEABLE FEAST

Ingredients

- Summer sausage
- Hard cheeses
- Crackers
- Pretzels
- Apples
- Dried fruit

- Beef jerky
- Fruit and nut bars
  (see recipe, page 103)
- Granola bars (see recipe, page 103)
- Gorp (see recipe, page 102)
- Dark chocolate bar

Directions

1. Fill your backpack with a moveable feast of tasty, high-energy foods that travel well. This mini-buffet is perfect for a trailside picnic.
2. Pack a cutting tool like a Swiss Army knife and a miniature cutting board for the cheese, sausage, and apples.

BETTER-THAN-SLICED-BREAD SANDWICHES

Ingredients

- Pita bread or tortillas
- Peanut, almond, or soynut butter
- Jam
- Hazelnut butter
- Bananas
- 1 can of tuna fish (with peel-back top)
- Packets of mayo
- 1 stalk chopped celery
- Salt and pepper
- Foil or big Tupperware container

Directions

1. At home, chop the celery and put it in a small plastic bag.
2. At camp, assemble sandwiches for the kids according to their filling and bread preferences. Sliced bread smooshes easily; pack pita bread, crackers, or tortillas instead. Our kids like almond butter and jam, or banana and hazelnut butter, rolled up in a tortilla.
3. For tuna sandwiches, mix the tuna with the mayo, chopped celery, and salt and pepper. Stuff tuna salad into a pita pocket (or roll it in a tortilla).
4. To carry sandwiches on a day hike, wrap individually in foil or store them all in a big Tupperware container.

Dinner

HOBO PACKS (SERVES 4)

Ingredients

- 1 pound ground turkey
- 1 clove garlic, minced
- 1 medium onion
- 2 medium carrots
- 1 red bell pepper
- Kernels cut from 2 ears of fresh corn
- 6 small red potatoes
- 4 tablespoons olive oil

- 2 tablespoons fresh basil, chopped
- Salt and pepper
- Heavy-duty tinfoil

Directions

1. At home, chop carrots and red pepper into bite-sized pieces. Slice the kernels from the corncobs and put in a plastic bag with the carrots and pepper.
2. At camp, chop onion and mince garlic. Cut potatoes into quarter-inch slices.
3. Lay out four large squares of heavy-duty tinfoil. Layer potato slices on each piece of foil, then top with veggies and garlic.
4. Divide the olive oil among the four foil packets.
5. Break up the turkey and divide it among the packets.
6. Season with fresh basil and salt and pepper, to taste.
7. With each packet, bring two ends of the foil together and fold them several times to create a seam. Then roll the open ends toward the middle, creating a tight seal.
8. Let your campfire burn down to hot coals.
9. Set the Hobo Packs on the hot coals and cook around 30 to 45 minutes, turning every 15.
10. Use tongs to remove the packs from the fire. Be careful of escaping steam when opening the foil.

ANGEL-HAIR PASTA WITH SUN-DRIED TOMATOES AND BASIL (SERVES 6)

Ingredients

- 1 pound angel-hair pasta
- 3 ounces julienned sun-dried tomatoes
- 1¼ cup shredded Parmesan cheese, divided
- ¼ cup milk
- ½ cup fresh basil, chopped
- 4 tablespoons olive oil or butter
- Salt and pepper to taste

Directions

1. In camp, put dried tomatoes in a small bowl, then pour boiling water over them. Let them soften for 5 minutes.
2. Drain the tomatoes.
3. Cook the pasta according to directions. (Angel-hair pasta cooks quickly, so it's a good choice for backpacking, too.)
4. Strain the pasta.
5. Mix the tomatoes, 1 cup Parmesan, basil, milk, and olive oil or butter into the pasta.
6. Season with salt and pepper, and sprinkle each serving with remaining shredded cheese.

Snack

HOMEMADE GORP (SERVES 4)

Ingredients

- 1 cup raisins, dried cranberries, or dried cherries
- 1 cup salted peanuts, almonds, or cashews
- 1 cup plain M&M's or chocolate chips
- ½ cup sunflower seeds or pepitas

Directions

1. Combine all ingredients in a large bowl, mixing together the salty and sweet components.
2. Change up the recipe each time you go camping by choosing different dried fruits, nuts, sweets, and seeds. You can also add sesame sticks, pretzels, cereal like Puffins or Rice Chex, candied ginger, or coconut.
3. Fill small snack bags with the Gorp and label with each child's name. That way they won't argue over who's picking out the M&M's and leaving behind the raisins.

IN THE FIELD

Ingredients

- ½ cup all-purpose flour
- ¼ teaspoon baking soda
- ¼ teaspoon baking powder
- ¼ teaspoon kosher salt
- ¼ cup dark brown sugar, packed
- 2 cups almonds, coarsely chopped
- ¾ cup pitted dates, chopped
- ½ cup dried apricots, chopped
- ½ cup dried cherries, chopped
- ¾ cup semisweet chocolate chips
- 1 large egg
- ½ teaspoon vanilla extract

Directions

1. Preheat the oven to 325 degrees. Lightly oil an 8" × 8" square pan.
2. Combine flour, baking soda, baking powder, and salt in a large bowl. Add sugar, nuts, fruit, and chocolate chips, and mix with your hands until the fruit is coated with flour. Separate any sticky bits.
3. Beat egg and vanilla together and add to the nut-and-fruit mixture.
4. Mix with your hands until everything is thinly coated with the egg mixture.
5. Pour mixture into prepared pan and flatten it down with a spatula.
6. Bake for 35 to 40 minutes or until lightly browned.
7. Let cool in pan. Using a stiff spatula, loosen the entire square and lift it carefully out of the pan and onto a cutting board. Cut into sixteen squares.

HOMEMADE GRANOLA BARS (MAKES 16 TWO-INCH SQUARE BARS)

Ingredients

- 1 cup rolled oats
- 1 cup puffed cereal (ideally unsweetened)
- ½ cup dried cranberries
- ½ cup raisins
- ¼ cup roasted sunflower seeds
- ½ cup almonds
- ¼ cup protein powder *(cont.)*

CAMP GRUB

- 1 teaspoon vegetable oil
- ¾ cup brown rice syrup
- ½ cup almond butter
- ¼ teaspoon cinnamon

Directions

1. Lightly oil an 8" × 8" baking pan.
2. Toast the almonds in the oven for 8 minutes at 325 degrees or until starting to brown. Stir once midway.
3. Coarsely chop the almonds.
4. In a large bowl, combine oats, cereal, dried fruit, sunflower seeds, almonds, and protein powder. Toss to coat the fruit. Separate any sticky bits.
5. In a saucepan on medium heat, combine the oil and rice syrup and bring to a boil. Turn down the heat and let the mixture bubble lightly for 3 minutes, stirring often.
6. Add the almond butter and cinnamon, and stir until smooth.
7. Add the wet ingredients to the dry and mix well.
8. Dump the mixture into the prepared pan, and press it flat with a spatula.
9. Bake at 350 degrees for 20 minutes.
10. Let bars cool in pan. Using a stiff spatula, loosen the entire square and pop it out of the pan onto a cutting board. Cut into sixteen squares.

Dessert

BANANAS FOSTER IN FOIL PACKETS (SERVES 4)

Ingredients

- 4 bananas
- 4 teaspoons butter
- 4 tablespoons brown sugar
- ¼ teaspoon cinnamon
- ½ teaspoon vanilla
- Heavy-duty aluminum foil

Directions

1. At home, combine brown sugar and cinnamon in a small baggie.
2. At camp, lay out four squares of heavy-duty foil.

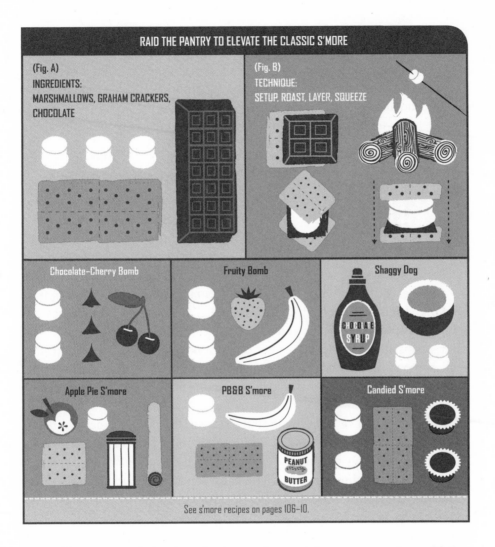

RAID THE PANTRY TO ELEVATE THE CLASSIC S'MORE

(Fig. A)
INGREDIENTS:
MARSHMALLOWS, GRAHAM CRACKERS, CHOCOLATE

(Fig. B)
TECHNIQUE:
SETUP, ROAST, LAYER, SQUEEZE

Chocolate-Cherry Bomb

Fruity Bomb

Shaggy Dog

CHOCOLATE SYRUP

Apple Pie S'more

PB&B S'more

PEANUT BUTTER

Candied S'more

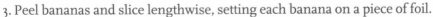

See s'more recipes on pages 106–10.

CAMP GRUB

3. Peel bananas and slice lengthwise, setting each banana on a piece of foil.
4. Dab each banana slice with butter, then sprinkle with the cinnamon-sugar mixture. Dribble a little vanilla on each.

5. Fold the foil to create airtight packets, but leave a bit of airspace around each banana, so the packets function like small ovens.

6. Let the campfire burn down to hot coals. Carefully set the banana packets into the fire and let them cook for around 5 minutes, longer if the fire's not too hot.

7. Use tongs to remove the packets from the fire and watch out for escaping steam when you open them.

SMART TIP Collect condiment packets from fast-food restaurants. Little packets of mayo and ketchup are much easier to carry than bottles.

Ultimate Camp Dessert: S'mores

The first s'mores recipe appeared in a Girl Scout handbook in 1927. It's a simple sandwich of graham cracker, roasted marshmallow, and melted chocolate that has become a camping icon. I've always considered marshmallows to be a tad lowbrow, which is not to say I didn't grow up on fluffernutter sandwiches and Rice Krispies Treats. But in ancient Egypt, the marshmallow, originally made from a pink-flowered marsh plant called mallow root, was the food of gods and royalty. They ate the root's sap with nuts and honey. That pedigree might help explain the delectableness of this classic campfire treat.

Just in case you've been living under a rock, the original recipe follows. Take s'mores to the next level by adding new ingredients and techniques. We raid the baking pantry and bring along handfuls of candy, cookies, dried fruit, candied ginger, chocolate chips, and nuts. With a buffet of ingredients spread out, the kids like to invent new marshmallow-based postprandial concoctions.

True chocolate aficionados will note that a Hershey's bar is only 10 percent chocolate; the rest is milk and sugar and "artificial flavors." We've tried substituting good dark chocolate for the Hershey's bar, but because the chunks tend to be thick, they don't melt as well as a thin Hershey's bar. We work around this by placing the dark chocolate on the graham cracker, then setting it on a pot lid near the fire or on the stove for a few minutes. Another solution is to use chocolate chips in place of the Hershey's bar. Ghirardelli makes a bittersweet chip that's 60 percent cacao.

THE CLASSIC S'MORE

Ingredients

- 1 marshmallow
- 2 graham cracker squares
- 2 pieces of a Hershey's chocolate bar

Directions

1. Set the chocolate on one graham cracker square.
2. Roast the marshmallow over the fire, until it's lightly browned on the outside, hot and gooey on the inside.
3. Put the marshmallow on top of the chocolate and top with the other cracker.
4. Gently squeeze the two crackers together, while removing the roasting stick.
5. Commit to memory the look of bliss on your children's faces when they bite into their first s'mores.

CHOCOLATE-CHERRY BOMB

Ingredients

- 1 marshmallow
- 2 dried cherries
- 3 to 4 chocolate chips or a small chunk of dark chocolate

Directions

1. Using a knife, dig a hole in the marshmallow. Stuff chocolate pieces and a few cherries inside. Be careful not to overstuff.
2. Put the marshmallow on a stick and roast.

FRUITY BOMB

Ingredients

- Fresh fruit (strawberry, blueberry, raspberry, banana)
- 1 marshmallow

Directions

1. Using a knife, dig a hole in the marshmallow. Stuff a bit of fruit inside.
2. Put the marshmallow on a stick and roast.

THE SHAGGY DOG

Ingredients

- 1 marshmallow
- Chocolate sauce
- Shredded coconut

Directions

1. Pour the chocolate sauce into a shallow bowl.
2. Put the shredded coconut into another shallow bowl.
3. Roast the marshmallow.
4. Roll the roasted marshmallow in the chocolate sauce.
5. Roll the chocolate-coated marshmallow in the coconut.

Note: Create a Chocolate-Bomb Shaggy Dog by stuffing chocolate pieces inside the marshmallow prior to roasting.

APPLE PIE S'MORES (SERVES 4)

Ingredients

- 4 marshmallows
- 8 graham cracker squares
- 2 Granny Smith apples
- 4 tablespoons brown sugar *(cont.)*

- ½ teaspoon cinnamon   • Heavy-duty aluminum foil

Directions

1. At home, combine the brown sugar and cinnamon in a small plastic baggie.
2. At camp, peel, core, and slice the apples into half-inch wedges.
3. Place the slices on a large square of foil and sprinkle with the cinnamon-sugar mix. Wrap the foil into an airtight packet.
4. Once the fire has burned down, place the foil pack on hot coals and cook for 5–10 minutes.
5. Place a few cooked apple slices on each of the graham cracker squares.
6. Roast the marshmallows.
7. Set the roasted marshmallows on the apples, top with second graham cracker square, and gently squeeze while removing roasting stick.

PB&B S'MORES

Ingredients

- Marshmallows
- Graham crackers
- Peanut butter
- Chocolate hazelnut spread
- Banana

Directions

Follow directions for the Classic S'mores, but layer it this way: cracker, peanut butter, chocolate spread, roasted marshmallow, banana, cracker.

CANDIED S'MORES

Ingredients

- Marshmallows
- Graham crackers
- Candy (such as Reese's Peanut Butter Cups, Andes Candies, and peppermint patties)

Follow directions for Classic S'mores, but substitute a piece of your favorite chocolate candy for the chocolate square.

ROASTING MARSHMALLOWS: FINDING THE PERFECT STICK

One of the most vivid camping memories etched in my mind is scouring the forest floor, through pine needles and leaves, over fallen logs and behind rocks, to find the best stick. You can go high-tech and buy telescoping, rotating, hardwood-handled, metal-pronged roasting skewers for marshmallows. Or you can make the act of finding a suitable marshmallow stick a campsite activity in its own right. Even though we have the metal sticks (my gadget-loving husband couldn't resist), I always insist we comb the area around our campsite for the real McCoy.

So, with a pocketknife in one hand and your child in the other, head into the woods to find the perfect stick. Here are some guidelines.

1. Look for a stick long enough so you won't roast your fingers, but not so long that you can't control the wobbly, melting mass of goo at the end of your stick. Three feet is a good length.
2. Choose a dry, relatively straight stick that's not oozing sap. Roasting marshmallows is already a sticky business.
3. To roast two marshmallows at a time, choose a stick with a small fork at the end.
4. The stick should be a little green so it doesn't catch fire. Avoid old, rotting, and potentially buggy sticks.
5. Peel the bark about six inches from the end. This makes the tool a tad more sanitary.

6. Teach older kids to whittle the bark-free end to a point using a pocket-knife. (Always cut *away* from the body.) The marshmallow will slide easier onto a sharp tip. Although with toddlers, a dull stick and a smooshed Jet-Puff might be the prudent choice.

CAMP KITCHEN CLEANUP

The sun has set, the family is pleasantly sated and snuggled around the campfire—and the dishes are crusting over with Parmesan cheese and rapidly hardening marshmallow.

The best outlook to have in this situation is to consider camp cleanup the same adventurous challenge as creating a tasty meal out of doors. You're not stuck at home scraping plates and loading the dishwasher. There are no counters to wipe down, no floor to sweep. Instead, you're surrounded by mountains and rivers, and breathing in the scent of pine.

Washing Up: Dish Duty

Many car-camping campgrounds have formal washing stations near the restrooms where you can bring your dishes and clean up a good distance from your campsite. If not, you can set up your own washing station at the picnic table—or as far away from your tent as is reasonable in an established campground. You don't want lingering food smells near your tent.

Use two plastic washbasins: one for washing, one for rinsing. While you're eating dessert, heat up a pot of water. Fill each basin with a few inches of water. Once the pot is boiling, add enough hot water to each basin to make nice warm water. Add a few dribbles of biodegradable camp soap to the first basin. The second basin is your rinse cycle.

Scrape as much food as possible off the dishes and into a garbage bag. We use a few baby wipes to remove any remaining food particles. Use a sponge with a scouring pad or a small scrubbing brush to scrub the pots and dishes. Rinse. Use a clean washcloth or tea towel to dry dishes.

If you're camping in a primitive site or the backcountry, be sure to wash dishes well away from your tent and at least two hundred feet from rivers and lakes, so the soap doesn't pollute water sources and endanger marine life. In the backcountry, you have no choice but to scatter the wash water in the pine needles—away from your camp and any water source, of course. At campgrounds, often the best policy is to dispose of gray water down the black hole of a pit toilet. Check with your camp hosts to see what their policies are.

Washbasins: Everything Including the Kitchen Sink

When it comes to cleaning up after a camp meal, despite my repeated admonitions about packing light, you might actually want to bring the kitchen sink. The simplest camp sinks are the garden-variety plastic basins (see above), but there are also high-tech, lightweight, collapsible sinks on the market. If you think you'll eventually backpack with the family, Sea to Summit has lightweight, collapsible nylon sinks that weigh mere ounces. The stuff sack on some camp kits also doubles as a kitchen sink. If you're really serious about dish washing, Byer of Maine has a car-camping wash station with polyester wash-and-rinse cavities and a mesh cavity for draining and drying.

Dealing with Trash

Camp refuse needs to be disposed of every time you leave your campsite (and of course at nighttime) so critters aren't attracted to the delicious scent of pancakes and hamburgers. If you have a large group that's burning through disposable tableware and utensils, you might want to use tall kitchen garbage bags for collecting trash. However, because garbage needs to get tossed so often, those small plastic grocery-store bags are the perfect size for camp trash, even for our family of five. Plus, we sleep better knowing that we have repurposed those plastic bags.

Leftovers: Limiting Food Waste

Calvin Trillin once said, "The most remarkable thing about my mother is that for thirty years she served the family nothing but leftovers. The original meal has never been found." Unless your portion calculations are impeccable, each meal perfectly satisfying your family's varying degrees of hunger, you will have leftovers.

Instead of tossing the fruits of your culinary labor, bring along sturdy, sealable freezer bags or airtight containers to keep leftovers. On a backpacking trip, we debated whether to bury or pack out leftover pasta. We decided to stow it in a freezer bag inside our bear canister overnight, with the intention of packing it out and tossing it. Amazingly, my son and his friend asked for it in the morning, and they both devoured enormous bowls of cold pasta for breakfast.

When you're car camping, you have the luxury of using the cooler for leftovers. Once the ice in the cooler starts to melt, consider double bagging food so the Ziploc full of leftover sirloin tips doesn't take on water. Ideally you can drain the water from the cooler and restock the ice every few days.

The Tidy Camp Kitchen: Discouraging Moochers

Leaving crumbs and food scraps around the campsite can attract little critters like squirrels, chipmunks, and mice. The Gray Jay is nicknamed the "camp robber" for a reason. While these animals seem cute, and many families are tempted to feed them, it's patently a bad idea. Encouraging animals to eat human food disrupts their natural ability to forage. Offering bits of hot dog bun to a ground squirrel is messing with its natural food cycle.

And it's not just Alvin and the Chipmunks who are after your food. Leave out the garbage or a food cooler, and you may attract raccoons or bears—animals that are not so cute when they're slashing through your tent walls to get the Snickers bar hiding in Junior's pocket.

Bears will most likely leave you alone unless they've gotten a taste for human food. Their sense of smell is a hundred times stronger than that of a dog. And bears are darn smart. If a bear has discovered food in a cooler,

SMART TIP

If your kids are easily frightened, you might consider ratcheting back on the bear hysteria. When you warn them not to sneak food into the tent, tell them it's to keep out skunks and mice. With certain kids, too much chatter about big scary bears will just freak them out.

CAMP KITCHEN CLEANUP CHECKLIST

☐ Plastic washbasins
☐ Sponge with scouring pad
☐ Small scrubber brush
☐ Biodegradable camp soap
   (e.g., Dr. Bronner's)
☐ Tall kitchen garbage bags
☐ Grocery-store plastic bags
   (for small amounts of garbage)
☐ Old washcloths or tea towels
☐ Paper towels
☐ Baby wipes
☐ Clothesline and clothespins

it will continue to associate coolers with food. So even an empty cooler sitting at a campsite might entice a bear.

At night and when you're away from the campsite during the day, always store food in the trunk of a locked car or in a campsite's bear box. These large metal containers lock and can easily fit an entire cooler plus bags of dry goods. If you put coolers or food bags on the backseat of your car, cover them up with a blanket or a tablecloth so they're not visible. Roll up car windows tightly. If a bear is able to squeeze its claws in a little crack, it can rip open a car door.

Never keep food, gum, cough drops, or even sweet-smelling toiletries like toothpaste, sunscreen, and bug spray inside the tent. It's best not to sleep in the clothing you ate or cooked in. Better to peel the chocolate-smeared shirts and pants off the kids, and toss those in the car, too.

Storing food in the backcountry, when you're miles from the trunk of the car, is a whole different chapter in a whole different book. There are many bear-deterring techniques you can use to hang a food stash, including using wires, poles, or lengths of rope. Tossing a rope around the perfect branch to hoist a bag of food is a tricky art. Some national parks now require backcountry travelers to carry bear-resistant food canisters, which don't need to be hoisted aloft. These oversized, scent-proof plastic jars have lids that are near impossible to remove, even if you do possess opposable thumbs and a big brain.

PART THREE
ACTIVITIES AND ADVENTURES

Emma looked up at the night sky. At home there weren't stars like this. Here, they were so bright they seemed to tangle in the branches of the trees. And there were zillions of stars, zillions and zillions of them. The full moon shone brightly, and when the tree branches moved, shadows danced.

—*Emma Dilemma and the Camping Nanny*
by Patricia Hermes

Chapter Five

OUTDOOR RECREATION

Morning's here! It's warm and clear!
Sheep load up their hiking gear.
Compass, whistles, drinks, and snacks
Go in packs upon their backs.
They trot along a hiking trail
Up the hill and down the dale.
Trees and bushes soon grow thicker.
Where's the trail? Sheep bicker.

—*Sheep Take a Hike* by Nancy Shaw

We were packing up for a weeklong camping trip, when suddenly my kids started to panic. They calculated the days, the hours, and the minutes they would go without playing Lego Harry Potter on the Wii, without feeding their Webkinz on the computer, without movie night on the big-screen TV. "Couldn't we just bring an extension cord?" they wondered. "A really, really long one?"

Sadly, they were not entirely kidding about this. What they didn't know is that there are so many outdoor activities you can do while camping, we wouldn't have a moment to think about thumb-numbing electronics and virtual reality.

On the following pages, you'll find activities that are site specific, like swimming and horseback riding. But most are outdoor activities you can

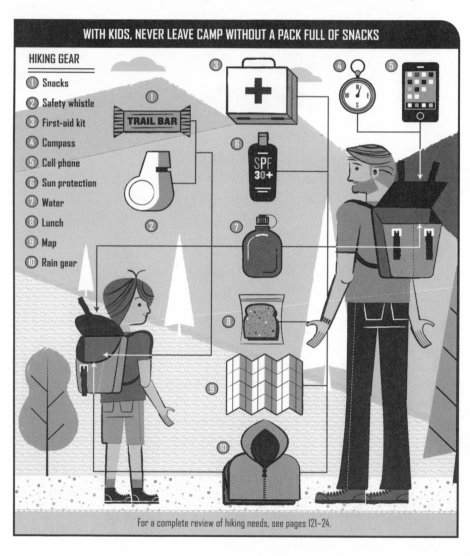

WITH KIDS, NEVER LEAVE CAMP WITHOUT A PACK FULL OF SNACKS

HIKING GEAR

1. Snacks
2. Safety whistle
3. First-aid kit
4. Compass
5. Cell phone
6. Sun protection
7. Water
8. Lunch
9. Map
10. Rain gear

TRAIL BAR

SPF 30+

For a complete review of hiking needs, see pages 121–24.

do anywhere, from hiking and stargazing to butterfly catching and geo-caching.

There are loads of ideas in this chapter and in the next two. But don't feel like you need to stack your itinerary with a half-dozen activities. Most kids, mine included, suffer mightily from overscheduling. Their days are routinely wedged full with school, soccer, baseball, ballet, gymnastics, piano, and homework. Half the joy of camping is just chilling out. It's more than okay to just let kids play. But just to be on the safe side, pick a few things to do for each trip. And try a few new ones each time you head into the woods.

HIKING

Hiking is the quintessential physical activity for a family camping trip. A ramble through the forest can be the most rewarding endeavor you undertake in nature. On one Father's Day camping trip to Peaceful Valley, Colorado, we took our three kids on a short bushwhacking hike along the river before dinner. It was completely spur of the moment, and we had no specific goal. The kids led the way, meaning we had to climb over giant tree roots, jump into sandy riverbeds (quicksand!), duck under branches, and squish our toes in black slimy muck. As the kids swung from branches across mud puddles, they invented Temple of Doom jungle names for themselves: Anya was Anya-ana Jones, Quinn was Quinn-iana Jones, and so on. When we got back to camp, all scratched and mud splattered, Quinn declared it The Best Adventure. *Ever.*

Hiking is the perfect time to teach kids to respect nature. In keeping with the Leave No Trace ethic, kids should leave plants and animals undisturbed, and pack out any trash. One caveat: once you train your kids to gather up bits of detritus on the trail, they'll be picking up empty cigarette packs and old cans in the grocery-store parking lot. Laudable behavior, but kind of gross.

You can also teach kids to reduce their impact on the environment by staying on the trail at all times. It's the perfect opportunity to introduce the term "erosion" into their vocabulary. And sometimes staying on the trail will mean walking right through a big sloppy puddle. Walking around puddles, you'll tell them, widens trails unnecessarily. Your children will love it when you urge them to get muddy.

Have kids carry a small pack as soon as they can so they'll become accustomed to it. Put only a few things in the pack: a water bottle, safety whistle, granola bar, and maybe a raincoat. You'll still need to carry the lion's share of the gear and food. You don't want to tire out kids unnecessarily.

And hiking can be very tiring for kids. But here's a thought on kids and perseverance: If children are properly motivated and they want to hike, they can go for miles. If they don't want to, they'll whine, grumble, gripe, and ask to be carried after about fifty yards. I swear it's about 80 percent mental.

On that same Father's Day trip, on the return portion of a hike to Beaver Reservoir, a pretty alpine lake surrounded by granite peaks, my boys started picking up large pine branches. "For the fire," they explained. I reminded them that we still had miles to go, and I respectfully suggested they ditch the sticks. "You're bonkers," I said.

Reverse psychology may have come into play, because the more I discouraged the stick carrying, the more determined they became. Aidan had giant hunks of wood under each armpit. Quinn dragged a six-foot pine bough for two miles, through dirt, over rocks, across streambeds.

But as any parent knows, even with determined children, a hike with kids is no walk in the park. In an instant, kids can complicate this seemingly simple endeavor. Legs get tired, tummies rumble, sunscreen drips into eyes, a special rock goes missing. When you're ready to hit the trail, start with these basic tactics for choosing the right route, distance, and timing.

ENJOY THE PORTABLE YEARS: Hiking with babies is not at all like hiking with kids. Aside from alfresco diaper changes, which can be tricky, hiking with a baby in a front carrier is pretty straightforward. Soothed by the motion of walking, babies fall asleep and parents can hike at their own pace.

Once kids hit the toddler years, they can ramble down the trail for a ways. As soon as they tire, you can hoist them in a back-mounted child carrier and keep going. I never minded this much, because I got more exercise from carrying the pack, and I could keep hiking on my own agenda, even when my child was too tired to walk.

It's when kids become too darn heavy for the backpack, yet not sturdy enough for an Everest expedition, that things get complicated. That's when you really have to recalibrate your notions about hiking and distance, and what makes a successful hike. It's time to enjoy the journey and not worry so much about the mileage and the destination. Type A personalities, this is when you need to take a deep cleansing breath and just let it go. In through the nose, out through the mouth.

ESTIMATE DISTANCE BASED ON AGE: A conservative guideline to approximating mileage is to figure kids can walk a half mile for every year of age. But this depends greatly on the child's physical strength and frame of mind. A six-year-old should, in theory, be able to handle a three-mile hike. Of course elevation, weather, the child's disposition, and energy level all factor heavily into the equation.

ESTIMATE TIME: Once you've chosen a trail of a certain distance, use guidebooks or trail-map times to get an idea of how long the route would take without kids. Many of those estimates are based on a pace of two miles an hour, adding a half hour for every thousand feet of elevation gain. Next, factor in your child's age, fitness level, and personality. Now take whatever time you figured based on those inputs—and double it. Maybe even triple it.

LOOK FOR VARIETY: Most kids would prefer a hike with changing scenery along the way: boulders, rivers, bridges, puddles, waterfalls, boardwalks, fallen logs. Avoid flat trails through exposed, unvarying terrain.

FACTOR IN ELEVATION: Vertical gain can work for you or against you, depending on your child. Two miles on a flat trail is considerably easier to hike than two miles with an elevation gain of even five hundred feet. That said, my kids find uphill routes more engaging than flat trails. They are more interested in scrambling up boulders and grabbing onto tree branches for leverage than plodding along a treadmill of a dirt path.

LOOK FOR LOOPS: Especially if your child thrives on novelty, look for a loop trail instead of the out-and-back variety. This way, the destination comes at the end of the hike, not at the midway mark. Many kids will balk at the idea of retracing their steps.

ASSESS THE TURNAROUND POINT: If you are doing an out-and-back hike, you have to take great care not to wait to reverse direction until the moment your kids are spent. Aidan once told me, very wisely and sternly, "Mom, I'm *one inch* past my half-way mark!" (What he was really trying to tell me was that he had a nasty blister on his right heel, but kids aren't always the best at communicating these sorts of things.)

SMART TIP

Sandals and flip-flops were never meant for trekking. Kids need hiking boots or sturdy sneakers with grippy treads. Slipping and falling on the trail can instantaneously zap the fun out of hiking.

TAKE A TOUR: If you're camping in a park with a self-guided nature trail, take it. Kids love finding the next marker on interpretive trails and taking a break while you read a little nugget about the surroundings. If you choose a ranger-guided hike, make sure it's one that's designed for kids. Otherwise, the children will be bored silly as a well-meaning ranger drones on about indigenous plants and geological history.

KEEP TABS ON KIDS: Kids love to run down trails. Before you start out, set ground rules about how far ahead they can go (or not at all). A good rule of thumb is to have kids in sight at all times. That means they have to be able to see *you* at all times. The downside to letting kids run ahead and out of sight can be serious. Children may take a different fork in the road from you and end up lost.

SMART TIP

Leave the camouflage shirt (the one that says, "I'm Hiding from My Homework") at home. Instead, have kids wear brightly colored clothing when hiking. It'll help you spot them if they run off.

TOP TEN WAYS TO KEEP KIDS TRUCKING DOWN THE TRAIL

Hiking is quite possibly the best family activity to do while camping. But it can also be the cause of anxiety and hand-wringing. If you don't play it right, a delightful walk in the woods can quickly turn into an excruciating trail of tears. You have to get tactical.

On a backpacking trip near Silverton, Colorado, I hiked with Quinn, then eight years old, to a ridgetop with a truly jaw-dropping view, the San Juan Mountains crammed to the horizon. We had slogged up steep trails for hours to take in the panorama. Quinn leaned into the howling wind, took the quickest of glimpses, and shouted, "We're going to die! Let's get outta here!" The moral of the story: young kids do not consider a spectacular view a worthy destination.

Following are ten tips for keeping kids content on the trail.

1. *Time the hike.* Most kids are at their best in the morning. And in many mountain environments, the weather is best in the morning, too. Set yourself up for success by timing a hike when kids are rested and well fed. If you hike early, you can be back at the campsite in time for afternoon naps, camp art, or card games.

2. *Dangle the destination carrot.* Start by choosing hikes with landmarks, like a bat-filled cave or a pond with a beaver lodge. Whatever you do, don't tell kids you're going hiking. Remember, "hike" is a four-letter word. Tell them you're checking out a haunted miner's cabin or skipping rocks in an alpine lake. It may sound like semantics to you, but to a child, it's a critical distinction that can set them in a positive frame of mind. To kids, the idea of exploring a ghost town or sticking their big toes in a waterfall is vastly more appealing than the idea of walking four miles in the heat of the day.

3. *Play mind games.* The homestretch on a hike is often the time to break out your arsenal of thinking games. One of our favorite giggle-inducers

is "Name That Tune." Trying to put a title on a tune takes the kids' minds off their tired legs. During one game, I hummed "God Bless America," and Aidan guessed it was the Pledge of Allegiance. So then I hummed the Pledge. The kids thought that was *real* funny.

For kids who are too young to identify a tune, just sing songs to pass the time. "The Ants Go Marching," "On Top of Spaghetti," and "The Bear Went Over the Mountain" are good choices. (Find lyrics and audio clips at www.kididdles.com.)

Other thinking games perfect for the trail: I Spy with My Little Eye, Twenty Questions, I Went to Africa, the Alphabet Game, and the Never-Ending Story. For more on games, see page 148.

4. *Play physical games.* One of our favorites is Hot Lava. The trail is covered in hot lava, and kids need to hop from rock to root to log to avoid having the soles of their shoes melted off. Have kids search for trail blazes, the colored plastic or metal trail markers that are affixed to trees. Make a game of collecting pretty fall leaves. Each leaf has to have a different shape or color than the rest of the collection. A hike is also the perfect time to do a photo safari (see page 177 for instructions) or just a simple scavenger hunt for the area's flora and fauna (see page 151 for instructions).

5. *Start seeing things.* Just as you can stare at the clouds and see sharks and turtles, you can anthropomorphize other natural objects, seeing animal shapes in inanimate objects in the woods. Thousands claim to have seen the Virgin Mary in a piece of cheese toast (weirder yet, that toast sold on eBay to an online casino for $28,000).

Start by lying down and staring at the clouds, the old-fashioned way, to find shapes in the cumulonimbus. Then as you hike, have kids look at other elements of nature to find animal and human shapes. Any shape, really. With a little imagination, you might see a dragon's profile in a big boulder or a bird's head in a broken stick. On one hike, my kids discovered a bird-poop splatter in the shape of the Nike Swoosh.

6. *Take breaks.* Relinquish your existing concept of hiking—you know, the one where you cover serious ground in a short time. Instead, stop often for snacks, water, rock tossing, or meditating by a burbling river. Take time to listen to birdsong, smell the pines, find the perfect hiking stick, or maybe just let the kids stomp on a decaying log. Pack a picture book like Margret and H. A. Rey's *Curious George Goes Hiking* or *Sheep Take a Hike* by Nancy Shaw, and stop along the way to read it. If you let the kids set the pace, you may not get very far, but you'll have more fun and they'll connect to nature in a more positive, life-affirming way.

7. *Split up.* Okay, so this may diminish the bonding element of a family hike, but everyone might be happier at the end of the day if one parent heads back early with a little one while the other parent forges ahead with older kids. On an out-and-back hike, the party that hiked ahead might even catch up with the group that turned back early. On a hike in Rocky Mountain National Park, my two little ones went on strike about a mile in. Instead of trying to prod them like stubborn cattle, I sat with them at a gorgeous emerald lake watching birds and spotting frogs, while my mother and my older son hiked another mile to an even more gorgeous emerald lake. They got their hiking ya-yas out; we had a peaceful and restorative break. Then we all hiked the last mile back to the trailhead together. It was the perfect solution.

8. *Keep topping off the tank.* Keep energy levels up by stopping for a healthy picnic lunch and plying kids continuously with ample snacks and water. Each child should have a water bottle or hydration system (the packs with water reservoirs and drinking tubes).

9. *Bring a friend.* If you're camping with another family—or if you're brave enough to take someone else's children with you on a trip—you may

OUTDOOR RECREATION

have more success on the trail. Having a buddy on a hike helps motivate kids, and they seem to whine less in front of their peers. Just like adults, kids chat along the way. They play and race each other and invent games with sticks and pinecones. All of which keeps them occupied on hikes.

10. *Employ bribes.* On hikes, bring a bag of M&M's or gourmet jelly beans. Organic 100 percent fruit snacks, if you insist. When kids begin dragging their feet or begging to be carried, start dispensing one sweet for every stretch of ground covered. I won't sugarcoat it (pun intended): this is a bribe. But when you still have a mile to go and your cutie-pie is squeaking like a rusty wheel, you go with whatever works.

STARGAZING

Beneath an inky black sky glittering with stars, my son Quinn and I cuddled down on a blanket, digging our toes into white sand so soft it felt like sugar. We were camping on the beach of Nebraska's Merritt Reservoir. The remote location makes it a perfect spot for stargazing. It's said the stars shine so bright in Merritt's pitch-black sky that the Milky Way casts a shadow. When you stare into a sky like that, you wonder if Henry David Thoreau was onto something when he said, "I have been looking through the stars to see if I couldn't see God behind them."

At the time, I was woefully unprepared to stargaze with my child. It was without a doubt a special moment, but pointing out the Big Dipper, I must confess, pretty much exhausted my knowledge of the cosmos. It's not that hard to brush up a bit to enhance your astro-gazing experience. After my daughter's preschool class studied the constellations, she taught *me* how to find Orion.

Here are some tips for successful stargazing.

PRACTICE THE DARK ARTS: The best time for stargazing is on a clear, cloudless night during the new moon (the phase when the moon is completely dark). You also want to be miles from the glow of city lights. By design, campsites are located away from light-emitting urban centers, making a camping trip the perfect time to scan the heavens.

USE BINOCULARS: Binoculars are a great tool for budding astronomers. For starters, you probably already have a pair. Binoculars are easy to hold, require no assembly, provide a nice wide view of the skies, and are less expensive than telescopes. Use binoculars to scan Orion's scabbard for the Orion Nebula, a giant cloud of gas where stars are born.

WISH UPON A STAR: Look for shooting stars, known to astronomers as meteors, which are really bits of space detritus, like rocks and ice, that burn up as they enter the earth's atmosphere.

KNOW BEFORE YOU GO: Before the sun sets, study the constellations with your kids and tell them the stories behind the pictures in the sky. *A Child's Introduction to the Night Sky* by Michael Driscoll has a glow-in-the-dark star finder, illustrated pictures of constellations, and accompanying stories. It's more fun to find Orion when you've seen the dots connected on paper and heard the hunter's mythology. Orion was forever having girl trouble—Artemis, Merope, Pleione. As retribution for one offense or another against goddess or nymph (depends on the story), a scorpion stings Orion, who ultimately succumbs to its poisonous venom. Regaling kids with tales of ancient mythology can make the constellations come to life.

START BIG: The Big Dipper, which appears in the constellation Ursa Major, or Big Bear, is one of the easiest to spot in the summer sky. Nearby is Ursa Minor, also called Little Bear or the Little Dipper. The end of the Little Dipper's handle is Polaris, the North Star. So, if you are facing the North Star, you know you are facing north.

LOOK FOR PLANETS: Often called the morning or evening star, Venus can be spotted on the western horizon shortly after sunset, or the eastern horizon shortly before sunrise. It's the brightest orb of light in the sky. Mars is also easiest to spot just after sunset. The red planet is identifiable by its rust-colored glow. And Saturn is a golden pinpoint of light you can see with the naked eye. Planets, however, can be difficult to spot. Orbiting the earth on

OUTDOOR RECREATION

their own prescribed paths, planets appear to roam among the constellations throughout the year. And at times they are obscured by the sun. One way to confirm you've spotted a planet and not a star is to watch for flickering light. Planets don't twinkle the way stars do.

SMART TIP Bring along a pack of wintergreen Life Savers so the kids can see stars in each other's mouths. In the pitch dark, when you crunch down really hard, you can see sparks.

MAP IT OUT: The night sky looks different depending on the season. Use star charts to know what to look for in winter, spring, summer, and fall. Orion can be seen in the winter sky; the Hunter constellation sets in spring, as Scorpius (not coincidentally, the source of Orion's demise) rises on the horizon of the night sky. At www.kidsastronomy.com, you can print out a star map for the month of your trip to help you locate constellations and planets. The interactive sky map at www.skyandtelescope.com allows you to view star maps for specific dates and hours of viewing.

STARGAZING CHECKLIST

- ☐ Binoculars
- ☐ Small telescope
- ☐ Star chart
- ☐ Flashlight covered in red cellophane
- ☐ Mobile phone with stargazing app
- ☐ Reclining camp chair, sleeping pad, or blanket

GAZE HIGH-TECH: Download iPhone apps like Star Walk, Pocket Universe, and SkySafari. These mobile tools use your phone's Global Positioning System (GPS) to bring up the night sky and label the view. Tap on a star, and the constellation appears on the screen. A dim red light lets you preserve your night vision. These apps also keep you posted on what's happening in the sky on any given night. If you own a Droid phone, try Google Sky Map,

SMART TIP

Bright light diminishes your night vision, making it difficult to stargaze. So douse the campfire. And if you're using a flashlight to read a star chart, cover the lighted end with red cellophane.

which uses the phone's compass and GPS to pinpoint your location. Point the phone at the sky, and it will identify the view in real time.

SPOT BIG BROTHER: As you gaze skyward, you might notice a star that appears to move slowly but determinedly across the sky. It could be an alien spacecraft, but more

SPACE JUNK GLOSSARY

Outer space is captivating to young minds. Astronauts, rockets, the moon, *Star Trek:* kids are fascinated by it all. You'll want to get your terminology straight when you're gazing at the night sky and identifying heavenly bodies. Herewith, an abbreviated glossary of space junk.

Comets: Icy hunks of rock and carbon-based compounds with fuzzy tails of ice and dust. In our solar system, large comets like Halley's Comet regularly orbit the sun.

Asteroids: Asteroids are small solar bodies composed of rock and metal that orbit the sun. Unlike comets, they don't have tails. Most are found in the asteroid belt between Mars and Jupiter.

Meteoroids: Chunks of space debris that result when asteroids collide, or when comets pass near the sun and shed bits of their tails.

Meteors: When a meteoroid enters the earth's atmosphere, it ignites, creating a bright streak of light called a meteor. Meteors are sometimes called shooting stars, but they are really burning chunks of space debris. Meteor showers result when the earth passes through the tail of a large comet.

Meteorites: When a bit of meteoroid makes it through the earth's atmosphere and lands on the planet's surface, it's called a meteorite.

likely it's a satellite. Hundreds of satellites orbit the earth, including the International Space Station (ISS), which is so large it shines brighter than Venus. Before you leave on a camping trip, plug the zip code where you'll be camping into www.spaceweather.com/flybys to see times and directions for viewing different satellites, including the ISS.

WILDLIFE WATCHING

There is a wonderful sense of discovery in seeing a deer pad right through your campsite. You don't get the same thrill when you walk on a paved path at the zoo, peering into small cages while munching on Dippin' Dots. Seeing creatures in the wild helps connect kids to the natural world. It gives them a context for understanding and appreciating animal life.

Of course, the nature of nature is that animals won't always be conveniently nearby. So pack binoculars to see a bald eagle soaring high overhead or a mountain goat scrambling up a rock face across the valley. Have an animal guidebook on hand to identify local species and learn about the animals you're seeing.

Many state and national parks provide animal checklists for kids, which make a fun game out of wildlife spotting. Kids are easily gratified by checking items off a list. In fact, some will go to great lengths to complete the task. During our Yellowstone trip, the animal checklist included the usual—bear, bison, deer, squirrel—but also the elusive wolf. One morning, Aidan woke up and insisted he'd seen a wolf out the window of the Old Faithful Lodge in the middle of the night. Despite the protests from his siblings, he checked "wolf" off his list.

IDEAL CAMP ACTIVITY: YOUR LITTLE WILD THINGS WATCHING WILDLIFE

WILDLIFE WATCHING

1. Field guide
2. Camera
3. Bug box
4. Binoculars and magnifying glass
5. Butterfly net
6. Journal

FIELD GUIDE

FIELD GUIDE

OUTDOOR RECREATION

For a complete wildlife-watching checklist, see page 136.

Most kids will object mightily to the idea of sitting quietly in a blind for hours in hopes of sighting the endangered Short-tailed Albatross. They just don't have the attention span or the patience for that type of contemplative wildlife viewing. Your best bet is to plan on observing wildlife you can count on. In Yellowstone, you're near guaranteed to see buffalo. In Rocky Mountain National Park, the elk are so ubiquitous they roam the golf course in nearby Estes Park. Watch seals in Cape Cod, sea lions in San Francisco, and Sandhill Cranes on Nebraska's Platte River.

SMART TIP

Make sure children stay a safe distance from wild animals. If it's a dung beetle, sure, they should get right up close to observe the bug rolling its little ball of poop. Use a magnifying glass, even. But if you're viewing large game like deer or elk, stay at least twenty-five yards away. Give bears a minimum berth of a hundred yards. According to the National Park Service, "If an animal reacts to your presence, you are too close."

When you do spot wildlife, remind children not to disturb or feed the wildlife. If an animal has to flee from a perceived threat, it uses valuable fuel unnecessarily. An animal might even leave a nest unattended if you frighten it. Feeding animals can negatively impact their digestive systems and encourage begging. Once animals get a taste for human food, they can become pesky, like the squirrel digging through our lunch cooler in the bottom of my stroller at the Denver zoo, or even nasty, like the seagull in Acadia National Park that made a kamikaze dive from the sky to rip a chicken wing out of my hand.

The stakes are even higher with larger animals. Real bears are not like Yogi. Once bears get a taste for the contents of a picnic basket and lose their fear of humans, they become dangerous to people and to themselves. Bears that boldly rummage through campground Dumpsters sometimes need to be euthanized. As the saying goes: "A fed bear is a dead bear."

Have kids keep notes in their nature journals about the animals they see (see page 184 for journaling instructions). The journal will preserve their memories and reinforce the delight of experiencing an animal in its own habitat. If you're lucky, a couple of randy bison may give you the opportunity to explain the meaning of "hanky-panky" to your toddler.

To help you identify plants and animals in the field, it's handy to carry along a small guidebook. Peterson, the National Audubon Society, and the National Wildlife Federation each have a slew of guidebooks for mammals, wildflowers, insects and spiders, butterflies, birds, and more. If you're just dabbling across the plant and animal kingdom, you may not want to invest in an entire library. Pick just a few relevant titles.

Another option is to download apps to your mobile phone. The beauty of a birding app, for one, is that you can not only read up on birds and look at pictures, but also listen to birdcalls while you're in the field.

Butterflies: Catch and Release

Butterflies are quite possibly the most enchanting insect known to children. Their wings are beautiful, they flit and fly like fairies, and they magically metamorphose from caterpillars. The best way for budding lepidopterists to study a butterfly is to catch it. Contemporary conservation practices discourage collecting and pinning butterflies, of course, but it's okay to use a net to catch and release butterflies.

SMART TIP Best times for viewing wildlife are dawn and dusk, when animals are foraging. Especially in summer, many animals rest during the heat of the day, making them hard to spot.

A horizontal, skimming sort of sweep with the net is more effective than swinging it downward like a sledgehammer. Once you've caught one in your net, clasp the wings gently together between your index and middle fingers. This way you can hold the butterfly firmly but without squeezing it. If your children are young, it's probably best for an adult to do the holding.

It's a myth that if you touch a butterfly's wings, it can no longer fly. But touching the wings does knock off some of a butterfly's protective scales, so you don't want to manhandle the delicate creature.

Enjoy looking at the butterfly for a short time: use a butterfly guidebook to identify it, make some notes in a nature journal, take a photo, and then release it. At www.kidsbutterfly.org, you can find butterfly facts, galleries of photos, and coloring pages for kids.

One of our longest yet most effortless hikes with kids was really a butterfly safari. It was a warm, sunny summer day, and the trail meandered through open meadows filled with wildflowers. We saw butterflies at every bend. With pink and blue nets bouncing over their shoulders, the kids never seemed to tire of chasing butterflies down the trail. When they caught one, the excitement was palpable.

WILDLIFE WATCHING CHECKLIST

☐ Child-sized binoculars
☐ Field guides
☐ Camera with zoom lens
☐ Bug collection boxes
☐ Magnifying glass
☐ Butterfly net
☐ Nature journal
☐ Pen and pencil

Birding

On a camping trip in southern Colorado, a gorgeous redheaded, yellow-breasted bird visited us regularly at our campsite. Thankfully our friend Bill, evidently a closet birder, knows his feathered friends. (The only species I know is the LBB, or "little brown bird.") Before long, the kids would shout: "Look, mom, it's the Western Tanager!" Although my son Aidan, king of the malaprop, sometimes calls it the Yellow Tangerine.

Birding with kids doesn't have to be a serious and intense exercise. It can be as simple as slowing down on a hike to listen to a birdsong or sitting on a log for a spell to watch a Northern Flicker poking its head from a hole in a weathered snag. While you're camping, take a walk in the woods or around a pond to look for avian life. Birds are often most active in the morning or afternoon. Wetland areas are perfect spots to sight large waterfowl, like geese and herons.

Encourage kids to sit still, listen, and observe. Have them notice things like feather color and beak shape. Ask kids to describe what birds are doing (perching, pecking, preening). You may be grooming future ornithologists. Have older kids sketch and label birds in their nature journal. Carry along a basic birding field guide to help identify species.

Bring binoculars to see soaring birds of prey or an osprey nest high in the trees. Eagle Optics (www.eagleoptics.com) has a multitude of binoculars and spotting scopes, as well as a kid-specific birding kit that includes binoculars and a field guide.

To help kids identify birdcalls, listen to sounds online at sites like www .birdjam.com before you go camping. Birders often use mnemonics to remember sounds. The Yellow Warbler calls, "Sweet, sweet, sweet, sweet-than-sweet," and the call of the Barred Owl supposedly sounds like "Who cooks for you?" You'll need some imagination to hear that one.

GEOCACHING: HIGH-TECH HIDE-AND-SEEK

A handheld Global Positioning System (GPS) receiver can be used as a navigation tool to help you find your campground in a fog as thick as a milk shake. But a GPS can also be used for geocaching, a family-friendly sport of sorts. Geocaching is essentially a digital treasure hunt, with more than a million containers hidden all over the world. Unless you live in the back of the boondocks, there are probably geocaches hidden right in your neighborhood, and almost certainly near your campground.

SMART TIP If you're not ready to invest in a dedicated GPS device, try downloading a geocaching app to your GPS-enabled smartphone.

Geocaching took off in 2000 when the US government unscrambled its satellite signals, making precision GPS navigation available to civilians. At home, go to sites like www.geocaching.com to download the coordinates and clues for a specific cache. Outdoors, use your GPS, the clues, and a map to locate the hidden booty. Geocaches usually contain a logbook and a collection of trinkets, from tiny toy frogs to wooden nickels. Rather than being buried in treasure chests, geocaches are hidden in weatherproof boxes aboveground. Geocachers are encouraged to take a trinket from the collection and leave a new doodad in its place.

Geocaching can turn a garden-variety hike in the woods into a pirate-plundering adventure. In the process, kids will learn the basics of GPS navigation. Although regular GPS units can run from $300 to $600, there are a few inexpensive, kid-friendly GPS models on the market that are specifically for geocaching.

JUNIOR RANGERS

Although my kids seem to thrive on novelty, I can already see that certain activities are becoming our family traditions. Whenever we go to a national park, our first stop is always the visitor center, so the kids can get cracking on their Junior Ranger booklets. Most national parks offer Junior Ranger programs to encourage young visitors to experience and learn about the park—and ultimately to help preserve it. The Junior Ranger motto is Explore, Learn, and Protect.

The programs are generally self-directed, with kids completing a series of activities in a Junior Ranger workbook based on that particular

SMART TIP Bring a clipboard along so kids have something to lean on in the field and in the car when they're filling out their Junior Ranger booklets. Use string and tape to tie a mechanical pencil to the clipboard. Regular pencil tips often break, and loose pencils disappear in the car's crevices at an alarming rate.

park, with different levels for different ages. Kids need to complete a certain number of pages in the book, attend ranger talks, and often fulfill other duties like picking up trash or spotting plants and animals in the park. Be sure to bring along crayons for the coloring pages.

Once they've completed the workbook and all the requisite tasks, kids can earn a Junior Ranger patch or badge, which is bestowed upon them with great ceremony by a park ranger. Newly sworn-in Junior Rangers have to hold up their right hands and swear to serve and protect. At Colorado's Black Canyon of the Gunnison, the park ranger had our kids also swear to listen to their parents and be good on the car ride home. When we get back from a trip, the new patches get sewn on their school backpacks.

FISHING

When kids are very small, a stick with a bit of fishing line and a small twig tied to the end is all they really need to go "fishing." Early on, we bought inexpensive toy fishing rods with reels and cranks and little plastic fish at the end of the lines. The kids liked them because they were covered with cartoon characters like Scooby-Doo and Batman. Children from around three through six will enjoy the simple act of casting and reeling in. They get to catch a fish every time—and nobody gets a hook in the eye. It doesn't seem to matter much that it's the same plastic fish time and again. At this stage, the sport is about how far you can cast the line and how fast you can reel it in. Bonus points for a hunk of seaweed.

As kids get older, they'll want to actually catch something, so you'll need to introduce real fishing rods into the equation. When it comes to fishing gear, there are infinite combinations of lines, sinkers, hooks, bobbers, swivels, poppers, jigs, lures, and bait. Here you will find the most rudimentary info on fishing. For more on fishing with kids, get a copy of *Boating Safety "Sidekicks" Go Fishing.*

In a nutshell, there are two basic types of fishing rods: spin-casting and fly-fishing. My recommendation for families with young kids is to forget about fly-fishing like Brad Pitt in *A River Runs through It*. Fly-fishing is an art that can take a lifetime to perfect. Fly-fishing rods are long, delicate, and expensive.

Instead, start small by using a spin-cast rod and tackle. For tackle, you can use either bait or lures. Essentially, bait is food, live or otherwise—worms, grasshoppers, crickets, shrimp, salmon eggs, hot dogs, dough balls, marshmallows, and so on. The best type of bait depends on the fish. (Ask for advice at the local tackle shop.) My husband and I once caught piranha in the Amazon with sticks, fishing line, and chunks of raw steak skewered on simple hooks.

The upside of bait fishing is the success rate. Fish can't resist a plump, wriggling worm dangling in their midst. Depending on the kid, a box of night crawlers from the tackle shop (or dug up from the backyard) can either be totally cool or completely gross.

SMART TIP Before your first fishing adventure, tape up hooks (or use a practice plug) and have kids practice spin-casting in a grassy area at the park or in a parking lot. It takes some coordination to flick the wrist just so and to let go of the button that releases the line at exactly the right moment in the casting arc.

If your brood falls in the latter category, consider fishing with lures—shiny metal slivers that are designed to look like shimmering fish. Spin-casting with a lure can be fun for kids, because it involves constant casting and reeling in. The continual motion can keep children's attention, even if they don't catch as much as they might with bait. With bait fishing, you cast the line, then sit and wait for a bite, watching to see if the bobber floating at the surface moves before you reel it in. Clearly, this approach takes a bit more patience.

Fishing is a great opportunity to discuss ecosystems and the food chain.

SMART TIP

Loud noises scare fish away, and children tend to be loud, especially in the wild. Kids are bad enough at using their indoor voices indoors, never mind outdoors. Choose a secluded spot to fish so you don't stress out about disturbing other anglers.

Especially if you're planning to fry up that trout. Use the time you spend untangling line and extricating it from bushes (and if you fish with kids, you will spend time untangling line) to pass on life lessons. If you're the philosophical type, talk to kids about the ethical dilemma posed by the sports of fishing and hunting. It's easier to call fishing a sport if you catch and release. Still, when you are trying to be delicate about ripping the hook out of a fish's mouth, your kids—whom you've always taught to be kind to animals—will ask questions like, "Daddy, doesn't that hurt the fish?"

SWIMMING

The beauty of swimming when you're camping is that it cools down and cleans off your grime-covered children. Most modern campgrounds have showers, but somehow that doesn't feel like camping to me, so we rarely use them. To plunge in a lake is to literally immerse yourself in nature—while simultaneously getting the stink off. It's a joy to swim without chlorine, and with a soft, sandy bottom instead of a toe-scraping concrete pool liner. Animal life can also enhance a swimming experience in the great outdoors. Kids can capture frogs, chase lizards, and search for sea stars. Of course, encounters with pinching crabs, stinging jellyfish, and the odd Portuguese man-of-war might have an adverse effect.

At sunset, you can sit on the shore and watch fish rising on the glassy surface of a lake. And if you were on a river trip with my family some summers ago, you could watch my five-year-old do a high-energy, foot-stomping, African-style dance while screaming his lungs off. He'd gotten some manner

OUTDOOR RECREATION

of biting insect stuck down his swim shorts. You just can't find that sort of wildlife entertainment at the public pool.

SMART TIP Remind kids not to drink the water when swimming in streams, ponds, and lakes. Microscopic organisms that cause waterborne disease sometimes lurk in untreated water. Although I wouldn't recommend drinking the water in the baby pool, either—think for a minute about all those leaky diapers.

Remember to pack bathing suits, towels, and water shoes if you're swimming in a lake or stream with a pebbled bottom. Even if the water's murky, pack goggles. For small children, bring along life jackets or water wings, but don't consider them substitutes for parental supervision. Even if your kids are strong swimmers, when you're around water of any kind, be vigilant about keeping children in sight. For more on safe swimming, see "Water Safety: Staying Afloat," page 224.

PADDLING: FLOATING WITH CANOES, KAYAKS, AND RAFTS

One of our most memorable camping trips was a float trip down the Niobrara River in the Sand Hills of Nebraska. The Niobrara winds through two-hundred-foot sandstone bluffs, past countless spring-fed waterfalls and stands of ancient Paper Birch. The river is wide, yet shallow, and the rapids are mostly riffles, so it was the perfect river for kids—except for the beer-guzzling partiers floating in giant inner tubes, but that's another story.

We rented a canoe and a kayak. For most of the way, one parent supervised each craft. But when the boys wouldn't relent, we let them (then aged five and eight) kayak together—tethered to our canoe. Anya, then three years old, slept in the canoe in a nest of extra life jackets. With the help of an outfitter who shuttled our gear, we camped on the banks of the river each night and floated beneath bald eagles and Great Blue Herons by day.

Whether you're in a canoe, a kayak, or a white-water raft, getting out on the surface of the water is one of the most enjoyable outdoor pursuits you can do as a family. Children love the novelty of floating on a river or a lake. It's hard to be bored when the scenery is constantly in flux as you glide along. Kids especially love wielding big sticks (a.k.a. paddles) and splashing their parents with them. Unlike with hiking, which comes to a standstill when kids run out of steam, when kids get weary on a river, they can just sit there for a spell and still make forward progress.

The first few times you try paddling with kids, you'll want to rent crafts from an outfitter. Depending on the type of water, your craft of choice, the length of your trip, and your comfort level, you might consider a guided trip. If you get hooked on paddling, you may want to buy your own kayak, canoe, or raft. At that point, you'll know more about paddling than I do.

Canoes tend to be bigger, with more storage room for gear. They have more stability than kayaks but are less maneuverable in the water and more unwieldy on land. Kayaks can be a bit squirrelly in the water, but easier to steer. Look for recreational kayaks, which have generous cockpits and wide, flat bottoms that mitigate rollovers. Big inflatable rafts, the kind used on guided trips, are great for family floats.

When it comes to paddling, a word of caution: canoes and kayaks are tippy, and kids are wiggly. With children, it's more than possible that you will roll over in a canoe or a kayak. When you're on a river, always wear life jackets, or personal flotation devices (PFDs). This needs to be a nonnegotiable

WATER-BASED ACTIVITIES CHECKLIST

- ☐ Fishing rods and tackle
- ☐ Bathing suits
- ☐ Goggles
- ☐ Water shoes
- ☐ Towels
- ☐ Personal flotation devices (PFDs)
- ☐ Water wings
- ☐ Dingy

SMART TIP

If you're canoeing, bring along a portable camp chair (the kind without legs) or a closed-cell foam sleeping pad. Set the chair or mat in the center of the boat for resting and napping.

issue when boating with kids. Also pay attention to water temperatures. In spring, the water in high alpine lakes is chilled by runoff from melting snow. In such waters, hypothermia can set in after just minutes of submersion.

When your kids are young, say from three to six years old, your goal is to search out flat water: easy flowing rivers, calm lakes, protected ocean waters. As with hiking, lower your expectations on mileage. On our Niobrara float, we took exactly twice as long as the outfitter said it should take to cover the distance. Kids need to stop for potty breaks, swimming breaks, exploration breaks. Take a deep breath and enjoy just being out there, surrounded by the natural world. Relish every moment that your child is delighted by dragonflies and gurgling whirlpools instead of thumb-pounding video games.

For most guided white-water rafting trips, age minimums fluctuate anywhere from six to sixteen. It depends on the degree of difficulty of the trip, which depends on the class of the rapids and the level of the water. You don't want to take kids on a river trip before their time. Getting ejected from a raft into a roiling froth of white water is not what you want for a five-year-old who's barely mastered the dog paddle.

BICYCLING

Adding biking to a camping itinerary ratchets up the gear factor. Your car is likely packed to the rafters already with just the basics, but if you can fit a rack on the back or on top and bring the wheels, biking is a great activity to do while camping. If you have smaller children, paved campground roads are the perfect place to tool around on a bike. In my experience, most cars inch around campground loops slowly, so it's a relatively safe biking environment.

If the kids are old enough to mountain bike, you might choose a campground near mountain-bike trails that are family friendly. Unless your kids are aggressive enough for steep, rocky singletrack threaded through the trees, look for smooth, wide trails over rolling terrain. Many hiking trails don't allow fat tires, so call ahead to find out what's available.

We've been on a few trips without bikes and regretted it. Yellowstone comes to mind: While many of the trails in the park are closed to bikes, there are a handful of paths that are flat, smooth, and long. Even when we were en route to emerald hot pools, bubbling mud, and exploding geysers, the kids soon tired of walking the flat paths. We realized they could have made those trips on their bikes in a sliver of the time.

If you have a small child who can't bike very far, bring or rent a tag-along (also called a trail-a-bike). This one-wheeled contraption with seat and handlebars attaches to the seat post of your bike. Kids can offer a surprising boost of power when they help pedal. Or they can just sit there like deadweight and get towed.

Don't forget helmets and consider padded biking shorts. Even little bottoms can get sore on a long, bumpy bike ride.

HORSEBACK RIDING

A trail ride can be a fun family adventure and a way to get into the woods without much exertion. Kids love horses almost as much as they love puppies. If there's a horseback-riding outfit near your camping spot, call ahead to find out the minimum age. Most operations require that children are at least eight to ten years old and can ride their own horse on trail rides. If you have small kids, ask about guided pony rides. Be sure to wear long pants so you don't chap your thighs. Close-toed shoes or boots, preferably with a small heel, can help keep feet in the stirrups.

The downside to guided trail rides is cost. Saddling up for a two-hour ride can set you back anywhere from $50 to $100 per person. Unfortunately most outfits don't offer discounts for children. (A horse is a horse . . .) That price tag can add up quickly for a family of four or five. But remember, kids love horses almost as much as they love puppies. So the price might just be worth it.

Chapter Six

CAMPSITE BOREDOM BUSTERS

It's campfire time. When stars wink from up high and sparks fly into the night sky, orange flames dance away the darkness. We snuggle closer and tell wonderful, scary tales.

Later, I listen to the night chorus of crickets and frogs. The lake softly laps us to sleep and I dream of camping.

—*When We Go Camping* by Margriet Ruurs

If you're a parent, undoubtedly you've experienced the classic irony of gift giving to children: you buy a giant and expensive toy for Junior's birthday, and the kids cast it aside and play with the cardboard box instead. You never really know what will spark a child's interest.

When it comes to camping activities, the best policy is the Boy Scout's motto, Be Prepared. As long as you plan ahead and pack toys, games, Frisbees, lengths of rope, maybe a coloring book, you'll keep the whole family engaged. Chances are the kids won't even touch your carefully crafted Bag o' Fun. Maybe they'll spend the weekend digging holes with sticks. And that's fine, too. Even better.

Following is a list of camp boredom busters that have worked for my family, ranging from active endeavors, like scavenger hunts and bat tag, to more sedentary activities, such as board games and reading.

KEEP KIDS HAPPY AND ENGAGED WITH CAMP GAMES – NO BATTERIES REQUIRED

Card games

Books

Sports gear

Board games

Bubbles

Bubble Time

Toys

For a complete campsite-play checklist, see page 149. For a complete quiet-time checklist, see page 162.

CAMP GAMES

Given a little free time and some imagination, kids will make up their own games. My son Quinn invented a game called Bess Hates Milkin'! It's a modern-day iteration of Purple Nurple, if you remember that sadistic game from your childhood. He starts out by asking unsuspecting players, "You wanna be Bess?"

On second thought, you might be better off sticking with the old standbys. Most of the thinking games that you can play in the car can also be played at the campsite: I Spy, Twenty Questions, the Never-Ending Story, and so on. Games that get little bodies moving while thinking are even better. Next time you're at camp, pass the time with the following nature-inspired games.

LEAF BOAT RACES: Find a mellow brook or stream near your campsite. Each person creates a craft from leaves, sticks, pine needles, bark, or grass. Any natural object found on the ground. (It's best not to use living plants.) Determine a start and finish to the course. On the count of three, players launch their crafts. The first leaf boat to finish is the winner.

CAMPSITE PLAY
CHECKLIST

- ☐ Frisbee
- ☐ Soccer ball
- ☐ Hacky Sack
- ☐ Baseball and mitts
- ☐ Soft football (like a Nerf)
- ☐ Lacrosse sticks and ball
- ☐ Little trucks with big tires
- ☐ Bubbles
- ☐ Sand toys
- ☐ Small dolls and action figures
- ☐ Favorite stuffed animal

BAT TAG: This game approximates the bat's use of sonar for hunting, so first you'll need to explain how bats use echolocation to find their prey at night. The game itself is better played in the light of day or at dusk. There are two variations to Bat Tag: the eyes-open version and the eyes-closed version. Depending on the kids' ages, the number of kids in the group, and the terrain around the campsite, you may opt for one over the other.

The eyes-open version is like hide-and-seek. One player is the bat, and the rest are tasty insects. The bat counts to twenty-five while the bugs hide. Be sure to set physical boundaries for how far the bugs can hide in the woods; you do not want to lose any bugs. The bat then begins to seek out its dinner by peeping loudly. Each time the bat peeps, the hiding insects make quiet but audible peeps

SMART TIP
To kill time on the road, play the License Plate game. One player picks a plate and reads out three letters. Next, all the players silently devise meanings for the letters (for example, 272-UUZ could be "Unbelievably Uppity Zebra"). When everyone has thought of a phrase, players take turns sharing. There are no winners in this game, just giggles.

back, creating the effect of an echo. When a bug is found, it becomes a bat and helps to find the remaining bugs. The last insect found becomes the new bat.

In the eyes-closed version, the bat is blindfolded, and the bugs continually move around the bat in a relatively close perimeter. Again, the bat peeps, and the bugs peep back. When the bat tags a bug, it goes to the bat cave (some predetermined spot at the campsite). The last bug caught becomes the new bat.

TWENTY QUESTIONS WITH A TWIST: Each player scouts around the campsite to find a natural object—a pinecone, a chunk of bark, a feather—and then keeps the object hidden. Taking turns, players ask questions to identify each hidden object. The holder of the object can answer only "Yes" or "No." The winner is the person whose object took the most questions to be revealed.

I WENT TO AFRICA: The first player says, "I went to Africa, and in my suitcase I brought home a _____." The player fills in the blank with an animal that starts with the letter A. The next player repeats the opening phrase, then adds an animal that begins with the letter B. And so on. Each player needs to repeat the animals in alphabetical order (aardvark, baboon, chipmunk, and so on) before adding the next animal (dwarf mongoose). This is a great memory game that passes the time in the car or on a hike.

At the campsite, make it a more active game by adding accompanying movements—chest thumping for a gorilla, arm waving for a pelican, a flying leap for a springbok.

FIRE STICK ROBBERS: Kids first collect several dozen sticks and determine a nearby jail spot. One player sits on the ground blindfolded; the rest of the kids lean the sticks against him, bonfire-style. Once all the sticks are in place, the children take turns sneaking up to the fire child and stealing a single stick. If the fire child detects movement, he points in the direction of the stick stealer. The child who was caught then goes to jail. The winner is the child who can spirit away the most sticks while avoiding detection.

SCAVENGER HUNT CHECKLIST

- ☐ Bird nest
- ☐ Bird feather
- ☐ Pine needles
- ☐ Leaf buds
- ☐ Leaf with smooth edges
- ☐ Leaf with jagged edges
- ☐ Tree roots
- ☐ Smooth bark
- ☐ Rough bark
- ☐ Dark rock
- ☐ Light rock
- ☐ Insect holes
- ☐ Flying insect
- ☐ Crawling insect
- ☐ Buzzing insect
- ☐ Spiderweb
- ☐ Animal burrow
- ☐ Animal tracks

SCAVENGER HUNTS

If your campground has a visitor center, check to see if they have a nature scavenger-hunt checklist tailored to the area. You can also use the generic scavenger-hunt checklist here or create your own. Include animals, insects, plants, and rocks, as well as evidence of animals: scat, fur, tracks, nests, and scratches on tree trunks. If the list is too long or you're short on time, have kids find only a certain number of things on the list.

Unlike a traditional scavenger hunt, you don't want kids to *collect* all the items on the list. Items like pinecones and feathers can be collected—then left at the campsite. Other items like giant boulders and lichen will obviously just get checked off the list. When in doubt, leave the scavenger hunt object in situ. This is especially

- ☐ Animal fur
- ☐ Animal scat
- ☐ Seeds
- ☐ Pinecones
- ☐ Yellow flower
- ☐ Decaying log
- ☐ Moss
- ☐ Lichen
- ☐ Dirt
- ☐ Dew
- ☐ Puddle
- ☐ Pond, lake, or stream
- ☐ Chirping bird
- ☐ Cheeping chipmunk or squirrel

important if you've got things like deer pellets on the list.

PLAYTIME

Be sure to toss in a few Frisbees and balls, depending on which sport your kids are into at the moment: lacrosse, soccer, baseball, football. Kids can entertain themselves for a good while with something as simple as a Wiffle ball or Hacky Sack. Leave behind the World Series baseball signed by Hank Aaron. Unless you're camping in an open field, balls will get lost in the underbrush.

If sports aren't your thing, then small toys can also provide entertainment in the car, at the campsite, or on the trail. On a camping trip to Colorado's Great Sand Dunes National Park, our friends were wise enough to bring along a handful of miniature monster trucks. As we hiked up and down the dunes, the kids let the trucks loose for high-speed races on every downhill. When we stopped for lunch, the kids built small hills and ramps, and rode the trucks around in circles. Okay, so they also bickered incessantly over who got the blue one, but otherwise these small toys entertained five kids on an all-day hike.

Bring just a few small toys for each child. Polly Pockets, tiny mermaids and fairies, pint-sized action figures and small dump trucks. Pack plastic cups or sand toys for digging, dumping, and making mud pies. Bring a bottle of bubbles—and enough wands to go around.

Of course, you'll bring a few favorite toys, but also bring a small brand-new toy for each child. When kids start to get wiggly in the car or while you're making dinner, the new plaything will be your shrink-wrapped secret weapon.

KNOT TYING

Tying knots is one part function, one part fun. Any Boy Scout or Girl Scout worth their merit badges knows that knots come in handy for tying off a tarp to a tree, lashing a bundle of firewood, or securing a canoe. But knot tying is also a fun bonding activity to do with your kids while hanging around the campsite. When our boys were just three and five, they sat mesmerized in their daddy's lap as he used a section of rope and showed them how the rabbit pops out of the hole and runs around the tree to create a bowline hitch.

Here are four simple knots worth knowing. You can find animated instructions for knot tying at www.animatedknots.com. The company also offers a knot-tying app. When you go camping, bring along a few short lengths of medium-thick rope for practicing knots.

Square Knot

The most basic of knots, the square knot is quick and simple. It's handy for linking two pieces of rope together to make a longer rope. If you can tie a granny knot, the one you learned to tie when you were six, you're halfway there.

How-To

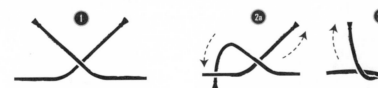

1. Take the ends of two pieces of rope. Cross right over left.

2. Twist the strands once, so the two strands are pointing upward.

3. Take the two ends again. Cross left over right, creating a loop.

4. Feed the top rope through the hole from the back and pull the ends tight.

5. The knot should look symmetrical.

Taut-Line Hitch

Use this knot for any line under tension that might need periodic adjustment. You might attach the tent's guyline to a tree with a clove hitch and use a taut-line hitch on the corner eyelet of your rainfly. When your tent goes all cattywompus on you, creating slack in the line, you can grab the knot on the taut-line hitch and slide it to adjust tension.

SMART TIP

When practicing with two ropes, use different colored ropes.

1. Wrap a rope around a pole, as shown. Leave a generous tail.

2. Drop the tail through the resulting loop.

3. Drop the tail through the loop a second time.

4. Wrap the working end under the standing end, creating another loop. Drop the working end through this loop and pull it tight.

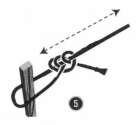

5. The knot will slide back and forth along the standing end.

Clove Hitch

This is a useful knot for tying a rope off to something, whether it's a post, a tree, or a pole. When we camp, we invariably use this knot. It's not designed for carrying heavy loads because it can slip, so if you're tying a Bobcat to a flatbed, choose a different knot. At camp, you can practice on a small tree, the rails of the picnic bench, or the arm of your camp chair.

How-To

1. Wrap the working end of the rope around a pole, bringing the working end under the standing end.

2. Wrap the working end a second time around the pole, above the first turn.

3. Pull the working end through the eye created by the second turn and pull it tight.

Clove Hitch Alternative

If the object you're putting the clove hitch on has an accessible end (say a post, not a tree), you can create the clove hitch an even easier way.

How-To

1. Create a loop with your rope as shown in figure.

2. Create a second loop next to the first.

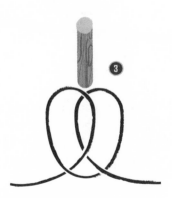

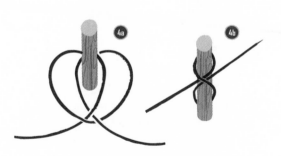

3. Place the first loop on top of the second loop.

4. Slide both loops over a post, and pull tight.

Bowline Hitch

This is a fun knot to teach kids. My husband says it's a good knot for showing off around the campfire. Because you are creating a loop in a rope, the bowline hitch is useful for hanging things like lanterns, bear bags, or water vessels.

It's easy to remember how to do this knot if you tell the instructions using the story of a rabbit, a hole, and a tree. Basically, the rabbit comes up out of the hole, runs around the tree, and pops back in the hole. Grab the tree and the rabbit, and pull to create a loop.

How-To

1. Create a small loop in your rope with the standing end (the tree) running vertically behind the loop (the hole). The standing end and the small loop should make a b-shape. Leave enough working end to create your loop.

2. Bring the working end of the rope (the rabbit) up through the loop (the hole), but do it loosely, so you create a bigger second loop of rope.

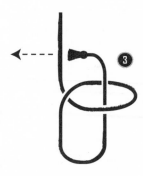 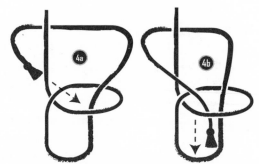

3. Bring the working end behind and around the standing end, right to left (the rabbit goes around the tree).

4. Drop the working end back through the original loop (the rabbit goes back into the hole) and in front of the second loop.

5. Pull the ends (rabbit and tree) in opposite directions to create the loop.

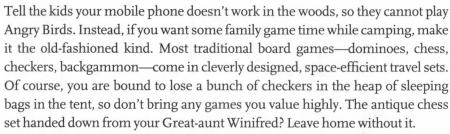

BOARD GAMES

Tell the kids your mobile phone doesn't work in the woods, so they cannot play Angry Birds. Instead, if you want some family game time while camping, make it the old-fashioned kind. Most traditional board games—dominoes, chess, checkers, backgammon—come in cleverly designed, space-efficient travel sets. Of course, you are bound to lose a bunch of checkers in the heap of sleeping bags in the tent, so don't bring any games you value highly. The antique chess set handed down from your Great-aunt Winifred? Leave home without it.

Look for portable chessboards that fold into storage boxes and come with magnetic pieces. A variety of models are available at www.chesshouse.com. Word games like Scrabble, Boggle, and Apples to Apples Junior come in travel versions, with snap-in pieces, zip-up cases, and hidden compartments for storage. Even Blokus, the popular strategy puzzle, comes in a travel size. Though I can tell you from experience, those little plastic pieces are darn easy to lose. In a pinch, you can always draw a grid on scrap paper and play tic-tac-toe.

CARD GAMES

Bring along a pack of playing cards to play the classics: Go Fish, Crazy Eights, Hearts, War, and Old Maid. Our family likes the new classics: fast-paced and adrenaline-fueled matching card games like Snap and Wig Out. In both games, there's no taking turns. Kids love the free-for-all aspect.

In Snap, you match color, pattern, or number in a battle of speed. (Don't tell, but it's good for developing brains.) In Wig Out, the cards feature sets of characters, each with a different hairdo. The idea is to create sets and add to them as fast as you can throw down. The first player out of cards yells, "Wig Out!"

Rat-a-Tat-Cat is another favorite. It's a slower-paced card game that employs math and memory skills, yet kids as young as five can play.

READING

Just before we embarked on a llama-trekking trip one summer, I stumbled across a picture book called *Is Your Mama a Llama?* at a garage sale. We all got a kick out of reading it at bedtime while a pair of 350-pound llamas grazed just outside our tent.

Most of the time, camping is a high-energy endeavor. Yet some of our most poignant camping moments involve snuggling in the tent reading books. It's the perfect activity for sitting out a rainstorm. Older kids will enjoy the novelty of cuddling down in a sleeping bag with a flashlight and a chapter book.

If you're organized, you can find picture books and chapter books related to camping and nature to bring along on your trip. In my life before kids, I would make a point to read a story set in my travel destination: Graham Greene's *The Quiet American* while in Vietnam. James Clavell's *Tai-Pan* in Hong Kong. The book brought the place to life and vice versa.

But you need to choose your books with care. During a trip to Brazil's Pantanal, I made the mistake of reading John Grisham's *The Testament*. While I was being munched on by Brazilian mosquitoes, I was reading about characters suffer harrowing bouts of malaria and dengue fever. It only made me paranoid.

The moral of the story: don't give kids nightmares with some sort of gory murder mystery set in a campground. Think twice about *Earthquake Terror*, a chapter book about a camping trip gone very much awry. See the resources section at the end of this book for a recommended reading list.

COLORING

At restaurants, coloring sheets are a godsend of distraction. Kids can be similarly entertained channeling their inner Picasso while you're cooking dinner over the campfire. Most kids would rather climb trees than color, but it's good to be prepared. Bring along coloring books, blank paper, crayons, and markers. Go online and Google "camping coloring pages" to find free, printable coloring pages with images of kids cuddling in a tent or fishing by a brook.

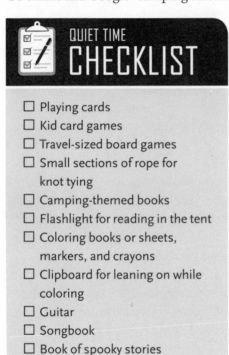

QUIET TIME CHECKLIST

- ☐ Playing cards
- ☐ Kid card games
- ☐ Travel-sized board games
- ☐ Small sections of rope for knot tying
- ☐ Camping-themed books
- ☐ Flashlight for reading in the tent
- ☐ Coloring books or sheets, markers, and crayons
- ☐ Clipboard for leaning on while coloring
- ☐ Guitar
- ☐ Songbook
- ☐ Book of spooky stories

MAKING MUSIC

When I sing, my kids tell me, in no uncertain terms, to stuff a sock in it. Everybody's a critic. But if you've got a decent voice and your kids are singers, feel free to belt away. Choose sing-along classics like "Kumbaya," "On Top of Spaghetti," and "Home on the Range." We like anything by Raffi: "Down by the Bay" and "Baby Beluga," to name a few. Bring a guitar along and strum through campfire favorites like Bob Dylan's "Blowin' in the Wind," the Eagles' "Hotel California," John Denver's "Take Me Home, Country Roads."

GHOST STORIES: SCARE THEM SILLY (OR MAYBE NOT)

My kids love ghost stories. The creepier, the better. My husband tells the kids the legend of an escaped mental patient named Three-Fingered Willy, a story told to him by his father. My stock ghost story is based on a true story about a young girl who was allegedly murdered by poison on her clarinet reed. Her ghost is said to haunt the band room of an old brick schoolhouse in Nebraska. If your kids love spine-tingling tales, get a book like William Forgey's *Campfire Tales: Ghoulies, Ghosties, and Long-Leggety Beasties.*

However, scaring kids out of their wits on a night when you're sleeping in the deep, dark woods might just be a tad unwise. Don't you think? Use your judgment with your own children. You don't want to make the stories so spooky that the kids are up all night.

Chapter Seven

CAMP ARTS AND CRAFTS

"To know and appreciate nature is the key to a lifetime of discovery."
My dad looked at me.
I looked at my dad.
"I know nature," I said. It was true. I watch it all the time on TV.

—*Alvin Ho: Allergic to Camping, Hiking,
and Other Natural Disasters* by Lenore Look

On a beach in Maine one summer, the kids and I collected old mussel shells, bleached lavender by sun and salt water. We smoothed out a section of the black-pebbled beach and created a sort of swirling starburst pattern with about a hundred shells. I'd been inspired to create something out of nature, right there in nature, by the work of British artist and sculptor Andy Goldsworthy. If you've seen his work, you know he creates absolutely stunning art by arranging natural objects like brightly colored fall leaves or pebbles in shades of white and gray.

My kids, ages four, six, and nine at the time, were totally engaged in the mussel project, as was my eighteen-year-old, college-bound niece. We spent over an hour fiddling with it. Next we created sculptures with periwinkles, rocks, and crusty red crab shells, sorting the periwinkles by hue to create Goldsworthy-like gradations of color. And sorting, as your child's elementary school teacher will tell you, is a great activity for little brains.

When we were finished, we took photos and left the creations for others to enjoy. It was a perfectly green project, too. We removed nothing from the environment, we purchased no supplies, and no greenhouse gases were released into the atmosphere.

Making art while camping, particularly when using nature as inspiration, can be a wonderful way to see and explore the landscape around you in new ways. On your next camping trip, plan to do one of the camp-art activities below. Some activities, such as pressing flowers and making twig frames, do require that you bring along a few supplies, but there are plenty, like our beach art and making fairy houses, that require nothing more than time and imagination.

LAND ART

This project is directly informed by the beach art I described above, which was very much inspired by the work of artist Andy Goldsworthy. Based on the instructions here, you can easily attempt this project when you're camping without any previous knowledge of Goldsworthy's work.

However, if you have the time before your trip, take a look at some of his creations, which are sometimes called land art or earthworks. This will add depth to this project and provide your kids with inspiration. Get a book out of the library on his work (*Passage* is a good one) or watch the documentary *Andy Goldsworthy's Rivers and Tides*.

Once you're outdoors, have kids create sculptures using natural objects found around the campground, in the woods, or on the beach. An integral part of this artistic process is that the creation won't last. An icicle star will eventually melt. White feathers arranged on a black rock will soon blow away. This art is meant to be ephemeral. It's a great opportunity for a philosophical talk with your kids about the transience of the natural world.

Materials

- Any natural object you can collect in the area where you are camping (leaves, twigs, rocks, pebbles, feathers, bark, shells, flower petals, acorns, pinecones, or berries)
- Canvas bag or plastic bucket for collection
- Camera

Instructions

1. Choose your medium (i.e., your natural object of choice).
2. Collect the items and choose a site to assemble them. A canvas bag or a plastic bucket can be handy for collection. Encourage kids to use natural materials that are not living (e.g., use pinecones that have fallen, rather than pulling cones from a live pine).
3. Sort the items by size, color, or shape. If you decide to use leaves, for example, put them in piles according to color. If you're using shells, perhaps group them by size.
4. Choose a shape or pattern. It could be a line, circle, square, squiggle, or swirl. Let your child decide. Establish a pattern within the shape. Maybe arrange the shells in a circle, with little ones in the center and big ones at the edges. Or create a gradation of color, with red leaves on one end, orange leaves in the middle, and yellow at the other end.
5. Photograph the final assemblage.
6. Leave the artwork behind for others to enjoy. While your photograph will serve to preserve the work for posterity, rain, wind, snow, and perhaps animals will deconstruct the actual work over time.

FAIRY HOUSES AND GNOME HOMES

A fairy house is a tiny structure built from materials like rocks, sticks, and leaves. This project will engage your child in nature and inspire magical play. Snuggled in their sleeping bags at night, kids can imagine real fairies, gnomes, elves, or wood sprites flitting about the miniature house they hid in the forest nearby. Kids use materials found in nature and they take nothing home, so it's an environmentally friendly art project.

Author Tracy Kane has a series of books on building fairy houses and a website you can mine for ideas (www.fairyhouses.com). If your boys think this project sounds girly, ratchet up the macho factor by calling the man-fairies Butch or Mack. Their house can be constructed for wood sprites or sparrow men. Or just call the whole thing a gnome home.

After our kids build these little homes in the forest, I surreptitiously tuck thank-you notes signed by the fairies and gnomes inside the houses. The kids are tickled to find the notes. It's "evidence," my littlest one says, that the creatures of the wood are real. It is a deception not unlike the whole Santa Claus subterfuge, but the look on kids' faces when they find the notes may be worth this temporary lapse in honesty.

Materials

- Any material found in nature, such as twigs, leaves, rocks, pine needles, flowers, pinecones, feathers, shells, seaweed, bark, grass, nuts, and berries.

Instructions

1. Find a spot in the woods that's secluded, but not so far from the campsite that your child might get lost. Choose a site at the base of a tree, perhaps tucked between its roots, or prop up your house next to a boulder or a fallen log.
2. Collect building materials. Encourage kids to use their imaginations; there are no hard-and-fast rules, no architectural plans. They could use sticks to frame out the house, stones for a pathway to the front door, pine boughs for a roof, flowers and fall leaves to add a decorative touch.
3. Remind kids to use natural materials that are not living. It's okay to build a

THOUSAND-YEAR-OLD ART PROJECT: CREATE AN INUKSHUK, LIKE THE INUIT DID

See instructions on making inukshuks on pages 170–71.

CAMP ARTS AND CRAFTS

house on a moss carpet, but don't uproot living moss and move it. Use sticks that have fallen rather than breaking branches from a tree.

4. The construction possibilities are endless. Fashion an A-frame from bark. Poke twigs into the dirt picket-style for walls. Layer sticks in a square to erect a log cabin. Or construct a house of stones, like the third little pig so wisely did.

5. Decorate the interior with furniture. A milkweed pod for a bed, a rock table, an acorn top for a sink.

6. Take a photo of the house and leave it for the wee people to explore.

INUKSHUK MAN

For thousands of years in the Arctic region, the Inuit people have been building *inukshuks* (pronounced in-ook-shooks). Inukshuks are a single upright rock or piles of rock, perhaps used to mark fishing and hunting grounds or the location of food caches. These ancient stones can still be found marking the barren landscape of the Alaskan tundra. An inukshuk shaped like a human is called an *inunnguaq*, which means "imitation of a person" in Inuktitut, the language of the Inuit.

Today, Canadians are known for building inukshuks along highways and hiking trails. In fact, the mascot for the 2010 Winter Olympics in British Columbia was an inunnguaq, and its giant figure can still be found on Whistler Mountain.

On a backpacking trip to Rocky Mountain National Park, my son Aidan built a rock man at the fork of a river. His own personal, giggle-inducing flourish was to add wet grass on top for hair—and name it Fred. He didn't know that the Inuit draped arctic heather on their figures to simulate tresses. For the remainder of the trip, we could glimpse, and enjoy, the little granite man from our campsite.

Materials

- Rocks

1. Find a flat spot to build.
2. Collect rocks of different sizes and shapes; rocks with flat tops and bottoms will be the easiest to stack. Your inukshuk can be hand-high or even knee-high. But remember, the bigger the rock, the greater the chance of crushing a pinkie toe or a finger.
3. Use a larger rock at the base for stability.
4. Set two similarly sized rocks on the base to simulate legs.
5. Next, balance several rocks on top for the body.
6. For the arms, use one long flat rock, or two side by side, extending out from the body.
7. On top of the arms, balance a round rock for the head. Choose this rock carefully. To the Inuit, this was the most important stone.
8. If the inukshuk is at all wobbly, use small stones as wedges to help stabilize it.
9. If you happen to return to the same camp in the future, go back and check if the figure is still standing. There are Inuit inukshuks that have lasted some four thousand years.
10. Take care not to build an inukshuk near a hiking trail that's marked by piles of stones called cairns. You don't want your rock man to mislead hikers.

Note: Toddlers can create a modified inukshuk by placing rocks flat on the ground in the shape of a person.

NATURE RUBBINGS

This project is incredibly easy even for younger kids, yet the resulting artwork can be truly beautiful. It's a magical process, as different patterns and textures materialize on the paper. Let your child guide the project by choosing

CAMP ARTS AND CRAFTS

the objects to rub. Leaves and bark are obvious choices, but hey, why not the cement slab outside the Porta-John?

Materials

- Sketch pad with sturdy white paper
- Crayons, chalk, or oil pastels
- Masking tape
- Textured surfaces
- Clipboard

Instructions

1. If you are using crayons, peel off their paper. Oversized toddler crayons work well for this project because they have decent surface area.
2. Place the paper on the surface of anything with texture—bark, rock, the picnic table. Either hold the paper for your child or tape it in place.
3. Holding the crayon (or chalk or oil pastel) on its side, rub gently across the paper, using back-and-forth motions, until a pattern appears.
4. To make rubbings of leaves, grasses, flowers, or ferns, place the plant on a hard surface, like your sketchbook cover or a clipboard. To bring out the ribs and veins on leaves, rub over the back side of the leaf.
5. Make a collage with different textures. Or rub the same leaf again and again on a single sheet using different colors.
6. Create a bark or leaf collection by rubbing different trees and their leaves. Add a scientific touch by labeling each species.
7. Protect the rubbings during travel by storing them inside a sketch pad.

LEAF CREATURES

A leaf is a leaf . . . unless it's an elephant. With a little imagination, kids can use leaves to create fish and turtles, peacocks and butterflies. They can even make little people. These creatures tend to look a bit alien, but invariably they are darling. It's best if you can collect fallen leaves instead of yanking branches off live trees. For inspiration, check out *Look What I Did with a Leaf!* by Morteza E. Sohi and *Leaf Man* by Lois Ehlert.

Materials

- Colored construction paper
- Glue stick
- Scissors
- 8" x 10" envelope or 1-gallon zip-top bag
- Leaves
- Sheets of clear contact paper (optional)

Instructions

1. Choose an animal or person, and think about what leaf shapes you'll need. Round leaves for a turtle's body, feathery leaves for dragonfly wings, oval leaves for a fish.
2. Using a big envelope or plastic bag, collect leaves, freshly fallen if possible. If the leaves are too dry, they'll disintegrate. If it's spring or summer, and nary a leaf is on the ground, gently snip a few leaves from trees, but leave branches intact.
3. Rinse any dirt off the leaves and press them under something heavy for at least half an hour. Longer if you have the patience.
4. Arrange the leaves in the shape of an animal or person. Combine leaves of different shapes and colors. Employ contrast. Maybe bright yellow wings on a dark green body. Use layering to create detail and texture, like the scales on a fish or the plumage of a bird.
5. Use small leaves for eyes, noses, beaks, and antennae. If you can't find the perfect leaf for these anatomical details, cut extra leaves to suit your purpose.
6. Once you're happy with the arrangement, carefully glue the leaves in place on a piece of construction paper.

7. So that the Leaf Creature dries flat, cover it with a piece of paper and slip it into a hardback book. Place something heavy on top.
8. Optional: if you want to preserve the artwork, place the paper on a slightly larger piece of clear contact paper. Cover it with another piece of clear contact paper, laminating it all together. You can find clear contact paper at craft, hardware, or education-supply stores.

BERRY PAINT

On one camping trip, though we had packed plenty of crayons and markers, my nine-year-old was intent on making his own pen and ink. Simply being in the woods had fostered a pioneer spirit in him. He found a suitable stick and some feathery grasses and used a long blade of grass to tie the "brush" to the stick. Next he made a big pot of mud paint and decorated the rocks all around the campsite. His determination and imagination were fascinating to watch.

Instead of mud, try making berry paint, like the Native Americans did. Of course, remind kids not to eat wild berries, which could be poisonous. The exception to this rule is when they are with you and walking through a patch of wild raspberries or strawberries. Wild berries are one of nature's most delightful treats. Native Americans made ink from the pokeberry, which is, in fact, toxic.

Better than building a paintbrush from scratch—my son's was not entirely effective—use the soft end of a feather or a piece of pine bough. Kids can also use sticks or feathers like quills, dipping them into the berry paint and scratching out campground constitutions, à la Thomas Jefferson.

Materials

- Berries
- Water
- Thick stick

- Jars or cups
- Feather, pine bough, or pointy stick
- Sturdy white paper
- Swiss Army knife or scissors (optional)

Instructions

1. Collect fresh berries. If you happen to find different colors, say blue and red, keep them in separate containers to make different colored paints. Or mix berries to make additional colors.
2. Smash the berries with a stout stick.
3. Add water a dribble at a time until you get the mixture thin enough to paint with. If it gets too thin, add more berries.
4. Using a feather or bit of pine bough, paint a scene or an abstract rendering on the paper.
5. To create a basic quill from a feather, use a sharp Swiss Army knife or scissors to cut the feather's tube on an angle, so it comes to a point.
6. Dip the feather quill into the berry paint and use it to draw or write on the paper. If you can't find a feather, try using a pointy stick.

PRESSED FLOWERS

Pressing flowers is a great camp craft—unless it lands you in the pokey. If you're camping in a national park, collecting natural objects, including flowers, is illegal. Even outside national parks, certain flowers, especially state flowers, may be protected by law. In Pennsylvania, it's verboten to pick a mountain laurel; in Colorado, the columbine is off-limits.

If you happen to be in a place where it's okay to pick flowers, you still want to follow certain earth-friendly guidelines. Pick flowers that are in abundance. Never uproot an entire plant; snip off just one bloom, leaving enough behind so the plant can continue to reseed and regenerate. Take only what you need and leave the rest for other campers to enjoy.

To press flowers, you can always go old school, slipping the flower between the pages of a heavy book and piling on more heavy books. Better yet, you can find inexpensive cardboard-and-paper assemblies with Velcro cinch straps. Using layers of cardboard and white paper sandwiched between two hard covers, these presses can flatten half a dozen different flowers at a time. These devices are simple to use and much easier to pack than your grandmother's *Encyclopedia Britannica* collection. Another tool to look for is the Sun Wave flower press, which uses a plastic grid to increase airflow and reduce drying time.

Materials

- Scissors or pruning shears
- Flower press (or heavy books)
- Clear contact paper
- Tweezers
- Glue
- Toothpicks

Instructions

1. In the afternoon, when a plant's water content is lowest, snip the flower stem a few inches from the bloom. Leave a few leaves on the stem.
2. Arrange the flower on the press's paper sheets, folding back the petals.
3. Place another sheet of paper on top, then sandwich the flower between the cardboard layers. Tightly cinch down the Velcro straps. If you're using a book, protect the pages with pieces of paper towel.
4. Add different flowers to other layers of the press.
5. Keep the press in a warm, dry place, like the trunk of the car. It'll take a week for the flowers to dry fully. Ideally you'll have consistent heat throughout the pressing process.
6. Back home, once the flowers are dry, carefully open up the press and remove them using tweezers.

7. Use a toothpick to apply tiny dabs of glue to the flowers. Affix them to a piece of sturdy paper for note cards or bookmarks, or to mount in a frame.
8. The craft possibilities for pressed flowers are endless: Sandwich the pressed flower between two sheets of clear contact paper for a place mat or window hanging. Glue pressed plants and flowers into your nature journal. Or use decoupage to decorate a wooden trinket box with pressed flowers.

PHOTO SAFARI

Despite the best of intentions, my two boys, and even my girly-girl, seem innately drawn to the prospect of shooting and hunting. Every stick in the woods is a gun. Every pinecone is a bomb. Rather than slingshots and bows and arrows, better to arm kids with a camera and let them "hunt down and shoot" things in the style of Ansel Adams.

This project has two parts: While camping, kids follow a shot list of objects in nature that you've drawn up ahead of time, checking off the images as they go. Back home, with your child, you create a small photo book or scrapbook annotated with journal entries from the trip.

The safari is engaging on two levels: kids love the instant gratification of snapping a picture and seeing the results in the moment (disposable-film cameras aren't nearly as fun), and they love checking things off a list.

Part One: Pre-trip Prep and in the Field

Materials

- Inexpensive digital camera
- Computer with Internet access
- Printer and paper
- Small spiral notebook
- Pencil or pen

1. *Purchase a camera.* Unless you're prepared to share your high-priced Nikon and suffer the indignity of fingerprints on your telephoto lens, you need to purchase an inexpensive digital camera. If you buy one that's more than $100, you'd be wise to also purchase an extended warranty so you won't freak out every time it slips from a grubby little mitt. We've used the extended warranty twice on our kids' camera. Your budget and your children's willingness to share will determine whether you can get away with one camera between siblings.

2. *Create the shot list.* You can use the generic list on page 180 or use it as a starting point to create your own checklist. Do some research on the Internet or at the library about the environment where you'll be camping so you can tailor the checklist to your trip. It's more fun to find a "hundred-year-old piñon pine" than a "tree." If the campground has a visitor center, use it as a resource to help kids identify obscure entries. If you populate your list with region-specific plants, animals, and geology, the photo safari will be an educational process. (But let's keep that intel on the down-low.) Make sure to include family members doing certain things: mom setting up the tent, dad pumping water, sister roasting a marshmallow, brother climbing a tree, Rover snoozing in the shade.

3. *Tailor the length of your list.* How many items you include depends on your child's age and the duration of your trip. You want it long enough to sustain interest, but not so long that they won't complete it. Hedge your bets with an optional "bonus" section. If they don't get to the bonus shots, they'll still be successful. For a four-year-old, maybe there are only ten items on a one-page shot list. For older kids, you might do a multisheet booklet of thirty items. Remember, it can take only a few seconds to snap a photo.

4. *Print out the shot list.* Personalize the list with your child's name, staple it together, and voilà! You've got a safari shot list.

5. *Keep a nature journal.* Okay, so technically this is a complete project in its own right. (See page 184 for detailed instructions.) If your child does keep a journal, you can borrow quotes from it for captions when the time comes to make a photo book (see part 2 below). If the children aren't journaling this time around, jot a few notes in a spiral notebook yourself. You can always wing it and go from memory to caption photos later. My journalism background combined with my pathetic short-term memory makes the notebook option essential.

Part Two: Creating the Photo Book at Home

Materials

- Computer with Internet access
- Credit card
- Blank scrapbook, photo corners, thin black marker

Instructions

1. *Make a photo book.* Like I tell my daughter when it's time to brush her teeth, you can do this the easy way or the hard way. Same thing with the photo book.

    The simplest, quickest way to create a photo book is to utilize an online site like Snapfish or Shutterfly. These sites offer book templates with slick graphic themes, as well as photo and text boxes.

    Once you've uploaded the photos from your trip, sit with your children and let them help you drag the pictures to the layout. Take snippets from the journal or notebook to caption the photos. In the absence of a journal or notes (we do not camp in a perfect world; maybe you didn't journal), let kids dictate *their* memories. Their captions may lack a certain accuracy, but they'll be more poignant. The older the child, the more he or she can do independently. Quinn, who learned to make a PowerPoint presentation in second grade, can create one of these books. It's that easy.

2. *Make a digital scrapbook.* If you're feeling particularly crafty, and you want a complex finished product, you can create a digital scrapbook to share online or print as a book. Digital scrapbooks are the middle road between the easy way and the hard way. For a list of digital scrapbooking sites, check the resources section at the back of this book.

3. *Make a traditional scrapbook.* This is the hard way, in my opinion. Have prints made of the digital images and then mount them (maybe with those little black photo corners) in a blank nature-themed scrapbook. Older children can pen corresponding journal entries next to the photos. For younger children, you'll be the scribe. (Overachievers: utilize your calligraphy skills here.) Then add memorabilia from the trip: the campground entry ticket, pictures from the park's brochure, a pressed flower. Use those little crinkly scissors. The reason I don't suggest this route is the same reason that my third child doesn't have a baby book.

Sample Safari Shot List

Campground

- ☐ The tent (outside)
- ☐ The tent (inside)
- ☐ Picnic table, set with lunch
- ☐ Family eating dinner
- ☐ Breakfast scene
- ☐ The campfire
- ☐ Roasting marshmallows
- ☐ Making s'mores
- ☐ Sunset

Plants

- ☐ Pine tree (piñon, ponderosa, Douglas fir, blue spruce, red cedar)
- ☐ Deciduous tree (oak, aspen, birch, ash, beech)
- ☐ Wildflowers by color (pink, white, yellow, blue, purple)
- ☐ Recognizable wildflowers (sunflower, daisies, thistle)
- ☐ Yucca
- ☐ Cactus
- ☐ Sagebrush
- ☐ Grasses
- ☐ Bark
- ☐ A green leaf

Animals

- ☐ Squirrel
- ☐ Chipmunk
- ☐ Camp robber
- ☐ LBB (little brown bird)
- ☐ Deer
- ☐ Beetle
- ☐ Spider
- ☐ Butterfly
- ☐ Dragonfly

Rocks

- ☐ Granite
- ☐ Crystal
- ☐ Red rock
- ☐ Giant boulder
- ☐ Pebble
- ☐ Cairn

People

- ☐ Camper in a hat
- ☐ Camper wearing sunglasses
- ☐ A hiker
- ☐ Sibling jumping off a rock
- ☐ Family setting up the tent
- ☐ Camper in a canoe
- ☐ Camper on horseback
- ☐ Someone fishing

Places

- ☐ Family in front of campground sign
- ☐ Visitor center
- ☐ Lake
- ☐ Stream
- ☐ Waterfall
- ☐ Hillside
- ☐ Mountain peak
- ☐ Cave
- ☐ Trail

Bonus Section: The Five Senses

- ☐ Sight: something bright, something dark
- ☐ Sound: something loud, something quiet
- ☐ Smell: something fragrant, something stinky
- ☐ Taste: something delicious, something unsavory
- ☐ Touch: something rough, something soft

TWIG FRAME

If you're superorganized, you could do this project at the campsite. Or you could collect the sticks while camping and create the frame back home. The twig frame can showcase a photo your child took during the photo safari, a pressed flower, a leaf creature, a bark rubbing, a berry painting, or a photo of your child's fairy house or inukshuk.

Materials

- 8 small twigs with branches intact
- Unfinished wood frame
- Polyurethane spray
- Pruning shears
- Sandpaper
- Craft glue

Instructions

1. Buy an unfinished wood frame. (Craft stores carry these.)
2. At camp, have children collect eight relatively straight twigs—four slightly wider than the diameter of a pencil and four about the diameter of a chopstick. Leave any small branches attached. Be sure to collect sticks from the ground, not from live trees.
3. Temporarily arrange your sticks on the frame. Using pruning shears, cut the twigs to size. Use the wider sticks for the frame's outer perimeter, the narrower sticks for the interior edges. Allow a few branches from the twigs to connect from the outside edge to the inside edge. Cut away any branches that extend beyond the frame.
4. To make the sticks lie flat, you may need to sand down any rough edges or knots.
5. Remove the sticks from the frame. Spray the twigs and frame with polyurethane for a protective coating and nice sheen. Let them dry overnight.

LET NATURAL OBJECTS BE YOUR INSPIRATION FOR CAMP ARTS AND CRAFTS

CAMP ARTS AND CRAFTS

1. Twig frame
2. Fairy house
3. Land art
4. Leaf creature
5. Nature rubbing

See instructions on making camp arts and crafts on pages 166–86.

6. Using craft glue, affix the twigs to the interior and exterior edges of the frame.
7. Frame your child's camp art.
8. Optional: for a different twig look, you can collect a bunch of small twigs and cover the entire frame with rows of twigs, parallel on top and bottom, vertically at the sides.

NATURE JOURNAL

Bring out the Henry David Thoreau in your child by encouraging them to keep a nature journal. When kids stop to observe their surroundings and to record thoughts and details, they slow down and connect with nature. Sketching a gnarled tree root or a brilliant bluebird preserves a memory that might otherwise evaporate over time. Years later, you and your child will treasure the resulting nature journal. Talk to your kids about Meriwether Lewis and William Clark, who kept notes on their exploration of the West in the early 1800s in a nature journal that remains treasured by naturalists and historians alike.

For kids, this project can be blissfully simple. (Although, surprisingly, there are entire how-to books dedicated to keeping a nature journal.) All that's really needed is a pencil and a notebook. It could be something basic, like a spiral-bound school notebook, or something fancy, like a hand-stitched Italian leather journal. Older kids can do this project independently; preschoolers can illustrate the journal, and you can record their thoughts for them. You can also buy a preprinted nature journal that includes checklists, journaling tips, nature facts, games, and activities. *Nature Log Kids* by DeAnna Brandt is a good one.

Materials

- Notebook
- Pen or pencil
- Colored pencils
- Pencil case

- Pencil sharpener
- Eraser
- Watercolors, water, and brush
- Markers
- Tape
- Field pack or backpack

Instructions

1. Pick out a journal at a craft store (or at a bookstore or even Target). Encourage kids to choose one with a hard cover that will hold up over time as it's shoved in and out of a pack.
2. Look for a book that will lay flat for sketching and writing. Spiral-bound books usually lay flatter than ones with sewn bindings.
3. While on hikes or just around the campsite, make notes about the natural world. Record observations about trees, flowers, plants, rocks, and waterfalls. Make notes on animals spotted, as well as evidence of animals: tracks, bird nests, fur clinging to a tree branch. Log what you saw, where you saw it, and when you saw it.
4. Remember to reflect on nature using senses beyond sight. Listen to the hoot of an owl. Notice the smell of a pine tree, the feel of its bark. Record these observations in the journal.
5. Write something each day and make notes at the time of observation. Relying on memory makes for foggy recollections.
6. Make sketches to accompany journal entries. Capturing a moment in time, images can be more evocative than words. Render sketches in pencil, colored pencil, or watercolor.
7. To create leaf pressings in the journal, apply watercolor paint to the back side of a pliable leaf, then put it onto your journal page. Place a second piece of paper over the leaf and gently rub it to press the image onto the page. Achieve a slightly different effect by coloring the back side of a leaf with colored markers. Label the plant.

BASIC CAMP ART CHECKLIST

☐ Inexpensive digital camera
☐ Pencils and sharpener
☐ Crayons and markers
☐ Watercolors and brushes
☐ Sketch pad, coloring sheets, loose paper
☐ Nature journal
☐ Glue, paper, scissors
☐ Chalk (for rubbings)

8. Tape bits of memory into the journal: park entry tickets, pictures of animals and plants from a park brochure, a pressed flower, and so on.

9. Use the journal not only when camping, but in the backyard, on a day hike near home, at the science and nature museum, or at the zoo.

PART FOUR

HYGIENE, FIRST AID, AND SAFETY

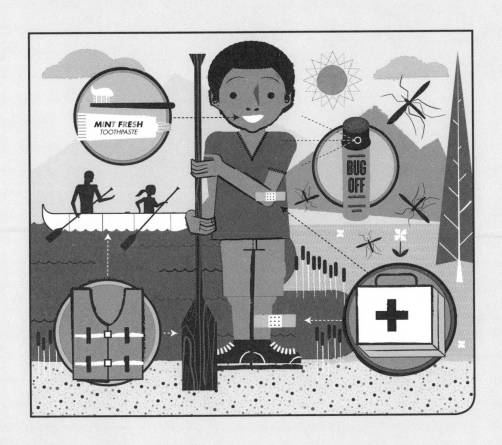

Do you know how to scare a bear?
Would you bang pots and pans?
Would you rattle some cans?
Would you shout? Would you yell?
Would you ring a loud bell?
What if that bear isn't easy to scare?

—*Scare a Bear* by Kathy-jo Wargin

"Real camping," said Pinky . . . "is roughing it."

"You grow a beard and live like an animal," said Eli.

"You either get hit by lightning or you don't," whispered Hobson.

"If you can't start a fire, you could freeze to death," added Scooter. "If you start a fire, you could burn to death."

"If you hear a rattler, it's too late," said Pinky. *"Sssssssssssssssss."*

"And when it's over," added Sam, "the angel of Death comes for you!"

—Alvin Ho: Allergic to Camping, Hiking,
and Other Natural Disasters by Lenore Look

Camp hygiene is a bit of an oxymoron. Getting dirty and even a tad stinky is half the fun of being out in the wild. It's hard to channel your inner caveman when you smell of Old Spice and Barbasol. As a child, the only time I saw my father with stubble on his chin was at the end of a camping trip. Maybe because it evokes fond memories of those trips, I like seeing that same woodsy stubble on my husband when we camp.

But when kids have been making mud pies and catching frogs, most parents will endeavor to achieve a certain modicum of cleanliness. You'll also want to maintain a few hygiene rituals, such as brushing teeth—especially if your little sweet peas wake up with fierce dragon breath, like mine do.

In this section, you'll find advice for staying clean and brushing teeth while camping, as well as best practices for pooping in the woods.

WASHING IN THE WILD

At established modern campgrounds, you'll find showers, flush toilets, and sinks. In the absence of such luxuries, you can keep clean enough with hand sanitizer, a washcloth, and some camp suds. And even if your kids are out of diapers, bring a container of baby wipes. They're great for wiping grubby faces and stinky armpits, not to mention a cheese-covered Swiss Army knife.

If you have a water reservoir with a spigot, set it up at the end of the picnic table to give yourself some running water. Put a bucket underneath to catch the runoff. Lather up with a bit of biodegradable soap—long enough to sing the ABC song—then rinse. (To conserve water, turn off the spigot while you lather up.) If you're out on a hike, wipe little hands with baby wipes and rub them with some hand sanitizer.

SMART TIP When it comes to changing a diaper at midnight in a nest of sleeping bags, a headlamp is infinitely better than a slippery Maglite flashlight between the teeth.

After dinner and s'mores, it's nice to heat up a pot of water and have kids wash their sticky, sunscreened, bug-sprayed faces and hands with soap and warm water. It's the camp equivalent of drawing a soothing bedtime bath.

I am not a clean freak, so I never worried too much about my babies missing a few baths over the course of a camping trip. But if you think your little dumpling will only nod off after a nightly bath scented with lavender—or if your baby's BMs tend toward explosive blowouts—you'll want to be prepared for a camp bath. Bring along an oversized plastic basin or storage tub (maybe the one your gear is stowed in) and fill it with six inches of water warmed on the camp stove. Use a washcloth to sponge off any dirty bits not immersed in the water.

Be sure to check the campground's policy for disposing of gray water. Some prefer you pour it down the pit toilet rather than scattering it in the woods. Don't forget the hooded bath towel with the puppy dog eyes and floppy ears.

DAILY HYGIENE CHECKLIST

- ☐ Antimicrobial hand sanitizer
- ☐ Baby wipes
- ☐ Moisturizing lotion
- ☐ Small tube of Aquaphor
- ☐ Travel-size deodorant
- ☐ Lip balm
- ☐ Toothpaste
- ☐ Toothbrush
- ☐ Dental floss
- ☐ Hairbrush
- ☐ Soap and shampoo
- ☐ Sanitary products
- ☐ Washcloth and towel
- ☐ Plastic washbasin
- ☐ Earplugs
- ☐ Needle and thread
- ☐ Contacts and glasses
- ☐ Prescription medication

BRUSHING YOUR TEETH OUTDOORS

If the campground has restrooms with sinks and running water, dental hygiene is a simple affair. But if you're camping in a more rustic area—or you just don't want to truck down to the bathrooms—you should follow backcountry guidelines for brushing your pearly whites.

At the campsite, dab a small bead of toothpaste on each child's toothbrush. Bring along a water bottle and walk to the farthest edge of your campsite (make sure you are well away from any natural water source). Wet the brush, then brush as per usual. When it's time to spit, you don't want to leave an unsightly, animal-attracting glop of toothpaste in the bushes. Instead, take a mouthful of water, swish, and—here's the fun part—try to scatter the frothy concoction over as much area as possible. It's the environmentally correct way to spray.

DOES A CAMPER POOP IN THE WOODS?

Defecation is a delicate topic for some, but the need to eliminate waste is an inevitability of life. And when you're camping, life goes on. If you're car camping, the best policy is to use the restrooms at the campground. If your campground only has pit toilets, you may want to bring a kid potty (see page 34).

Of course, it's likely that you'll be out on a hike when someone needs to answer the call of nature. And mark my words, you'll be miles down the trail when your little honey-bunny will announce, "I've gotta poop . . . *real bad*!" If your kids are like mine, they will wait to the last possible second to make this sort of pronouncement. You need to be ready for a backcountry squat at a moment's notice. Be prepared by bringing a plastic poop shovel or small garden trowel, a plastic bag filled with toilet paper or baby wipes, a sturdy sealable plastic bag for trash, and some hand sanitizer.

Peeing is pretty simple. Just find a spot with a little privacy, behind a rock or a tree, at least two hundred feet from streams and lakes. (For most adults, that's seventy paces.) When it comes to Number Two, you need to follow a certain protocol. Find a private spot at least two hundred feet from any water sources, hiking trails, or campsites. When you're camping, you never want to poop in your own backyard—or your neighbor's.

It's important to bury solid human waste because it can pollute water and spread disease. Using the little shovel, dig a cat hole six to eight inches deep. Squat and deposit. Cover up the poop with the

SMART TIP

Even in the wild, you need to clean up after your pooch. Nobody wants to trek past a steaming pile of doggie doo. This is a fact. Bring along a bunch of plastic bags for scooping poop, packing it out, and getting it into a campground Dumpster.

SMART TIP

Become an expert on eliminating waste in the great outdoors with Kathleen Meyer's *How to Shit in the Woods*, a surprisingly thoughtful, thorough, and well-written treatise on the subject.

dirt you dug out of the hole and conceal it with sticks, leaves, or rocks. Put the toilet paper in your sealable plastic bag so you can pack it out. Also pack out any baby wipes and sanitary products.

If you're hiking or camping with an infant, you'll need to bring along the diaper bag and all the requisite wipes and creams. Those changing pads that fold up and tuck into the diaper bag are especially helpful for backcountry changes. You don't really want to lay down your bambino's precious tushy in the dirt, do you? Roll up the wipes in the diaper and pack it all out. Dirty nappies will not biodegrade in a cat hole anytime soon.

In deserts, arctic landscapes, high alpine environments, or in river corridors,

BACKWOODS POTTYING CHECKLIST

- ☐ Small poop shovel or garden trowel
- ☐ Toilet paper or baby wipes in a plastic bag
- ☐ Diaper-rash cream for babies
- ☐ Plastic bag for trash
- ☐ Hand sanitizer

you may be required to pack *all* your waste out. Check with the land manager where you're camping for local regulations. If that's the case, you'll want to look into pack-it-out systems called WAG bags (WAG stands for "Waste Alleviation and Gelling"), which come with "poo powder" to help manage the mess. The whole business sounds pretty unsavory, but it's not that much different from picking up after your dog—something many folks do on a daily basis.

DAILY HYGIENE

Chapter Nine
ACHES, PAINS, PESKY PLANTS, AND BUGS

"Look!" Stanley pointed at the vine.

"Great find, Stanley! See, your Boy Scout skills have come in handy."

"Those leaves look familiar," said Stanley, "but I can't remember why."

Each leaf had three points and there were plenty of them. We picked and picked until we filled up the sack.

—*Piper Reed, Campfire Girl* by Kimberly Willis Holt

This is a true cautionary tale. My older sister, Cathy, was out for a jog along the quiet back roads of Long Island's bucolic North Shore when nature called. She hadn't planned on squatting in the woods, so she had no toilet paper. When the time came, she just grabbed a bunch of leaves and wiped. Can you guess where this is going? The leaves were poison ivy, a.k.a. *Toxicodendron radicans.* You can only imagine the level of discomfort caused by an itchy rash in your nether regions.

Now, Cathy wasn't camping when this most unfortunate event occurred, but the moral of the story still applies: leaves of three, let it be. (PS: My brother Steve would also advise against weed whacking poison ivy while wearing shorts, but hopefully you won't be battling weeds while on vacation.)

Other sage advice you'll find in this chapter includes how to defend yourself from all manner of biting and stinging insects, how to protect your feet from blisters, and the importance of bringing a well-stocked first-aid kit to treat minor aches, pains, itchy bits, and boo-boos in general.

Disclaimer: I am not a doctor. Nor am I a nurse, a rescue worker, or an EMT. My CPR training is out-of-date. I have, however, watched a fair share of *ER* episodes, mostly the ones with George Clooney. Use your own best judgment when you're camping and consult real experts when necessary.

POISONOUS PLANTS: LEAVES OF THREE, LET IT BE

Poison ivy has three shiny green leaves, with large serrations at the edges. It grows as a vine or a bush, turns red in fall, and at times has white berries. A helpful saying: "Berries white, take flight."

Poison oak looks similar to poison ivy, though its leaves are shaped more like oak leaves, which have rounded lobes. Poison ivy and poison oak can grow in thick hairy vines, so also teach your kids the phrase: "Hairy rope? Don't be a dope."

Also keep an eye out for poison sumac. This plant is in the same plant family as poison ivy, but its oval-shaped leaves grow in bunches of seven to thirteen.

Contact with urushiol (you-ROO-shee-ol), the oil found in poison ivy, poison oak, and poison sumac, can cause an itchy allergic rash of red bumps, streaks, and blisters. Reactions can vary. A rash might show up anywhere from several hours to several days later. Most people will get a mild rash; severe cases may require hospitalization. It only takes one nanogram, or a billionth of a gram, of urushiol to cause a rash.

Before you go camping, search Google images to show your kids what poison ivy and its relatives look like. Or get a book out of the library. Once you can identify the noxious plants, point them out to kids every time you see them, so they learn to recognize the plants and avoid them.

DON'T USE THESE PLANTS FOR YOUR LEAF-RUBBING CRAFT

Long pants, long sleeves, and boots can protect you from poisonous plants.

HYDROCORTISONE

Poison sumac

Poison oak

Poison ivy

For a review of poisonous plants, see pages 196 and 198.

SMART TIP It's a myth that the blister fluid from a poison-ivy rash is contagious. Although it is true that poison-ivy oil remaining on the skin could spread elsewhere on the body or be passed on to a friend. Similarly, if your dog has been rolling in poison ivy, it can transfer the oil to you.

Long sleeves, long pants, and close-toed shoes can help protect against poison ivy, but they are not guaranteed barriers because the offending oil can still leak through. The best defense, however, is offense: Scan the trailside for poison ivy as you're hiking. At break times, teach kids to study the ground before they plop their rumps into the undergrowth.

If anyone in the family gets exposed, you have about a ten-minute window before the oil absorbs into the skin. Wash the affected site with cold water (don't use hot; it opens up the pores) or swab the area with alcohol to remove the oil. Avoid soap, which can spread the oil. Remove any clothing and put it in a plastic bag to bring home and wash. You can get a rash from touching clothing contaminated with the plant's oil. If you do get a rash, a 1 percent hydrocortisone ointment can help relieve the itching. Of course, if you or your child reacts severely to poison ivy, seek medical attention immediately.

MOSQUITOES, TICKS, AND BEES

Flying, buzzing, and biting insects are a fact of nature, and they're hard to avoid when you're spending time 24/7 in nature. In addition to causing itchy bites, mosquitoes in the United States can also transmit West Nile virus, a sometimes serious disease that can result in encephalitis and meningitis. Ticks can transmit Lyme disease and Rocky Mountain spotted fever.

Ticks in particular are nasty little bloodsuckers. I once made the mistake of using a microscope to look at a tick burrowed into my lower leg. You really don't want to see a tick at that kind of magnification. Still, try not to freak out about ticks. An infected tick—and not all ticks are infected—would need to be slurping your blood for thirty-six to forty-eight hours to transmit Lyme disease. And you're unlikely to contract Rocky Mountain spotted fever unless a tick remains attached upwards of ten hours. Probably more like twenty. Ticks tend to hang out on your person for hours before they start feeding and, subsequently, transmitting disease.

After a bushwhacking adventure in the woods and certainly before bedtime, do full-body tick checks on the whole family. Be sure to scan the hair, knees, armpits, belly button, groin, and behind the ears. Ticks can be as big as a split pea or as small as a poppy seed. As long as you check regularly for hitchhikers, chances of staying disease-free are good.

There are plenty of evasive tactics for dealing with bothersome bugs and reducing your chances of contracting an arthropod-transmitted disease. Fend off irksome bugs by following the steps below.

- Don't camp near swamps, marshes, or other water sources. Skeeters and blackflies congregate around water.
- Wear long sleeves, long pants, and close-toed shoes at dawn and dusk, when mosquitoes are most active.
- Use insect repellent, especially in known mosquito- and tick-infested areas.
- When hiking in tall grass, tuck pants into socks and liberally squirt bug repellent onto your clothing from the knees down to combat ticks and chiggers.
- If you're more worried about ticks than dirt, have children wear light-colored clothing, which makes it easier to spot the creepy crawlies and is less attractive to mosquitoes.
- Avoid wearing perfume or fragrance-laced body products, which can attract insects.
- At the campsite, build a fire to ward off bugs.
- Always zip up the tent door, even if you're heading back out in a few minutes, and flip off the flashlight when the door is open.

- If you're in a superbuggy environment, a screened-in shelter can serve as a refuge.

Insect Repellents: Chemical vs. Natural

Insect repellents with a high concentration of DEET are by far the most effective, long-lasting defense against mosquitoes, as well as ticks, biting flies, chiggers, and other pesky bugs. A study in the *New England Journal of Medicine* comparing the efficacy of different insect repellents showed that a formulation with 23 percent DEET will protect you for five hours against mosquitoes. In contrast, formulations with citronella repelled mosquitoes for only twenty minutes. The best natural repellent in the study was a soy-based bug repellent called BiteBlocker. It protected against mosquitoes for an hour and a half—longer than kid-specific formulations with 4.75 percent DEET.[1]

SMART TIP

The CDC warns against products that combine sunscreen and DEET-based insect repellents. Sunscreen should be applied and reapplied liberally; insect repellents with DEET should not. Using a combination formula could expose you to unnecessarily high amounts of DEET. Researchers have found that in formulations combining sunscreen and insect repellent, the DEET absorbs into the skin more than three times faster than when DEET is used alone.[2]

Although DEET is a proven repellent, it's also a toxic chemical with potentially harmful side effects. You might not want to slather it all over your little lovelies. The Healthy Child Healthy World organization warns never to use DEET on infants less than two months; for older children, they recommend using concentrations of 10 percent or less. Regardless of the concentration level, never spray DEET near kids' faces or on their hands (which they will undoubtedly stuff into their mouths). And don't let children apply repellents themselves.

More natural choices are repellents with soybean oil, eucalyptus, and citronella, though products with these ingredients don't provide the same long-lasting protection against biting insects as high concentrations of DEET. Natural repellents can be, and likely need to be, applied more frequently.

The same study in the *New England Journal of Medicine* found that repellents with oil of eucalyptus protected subjects for a respectable two hours. Long enough that in 2008 the Centers for Disease Control and Prevention (CDC) included oil of lemon eucalyptus on its short list of approved insect repellents. It did caution that these products are not recommended for children under three.[3]

SMART TIP Rather than squirting bug spray near children's eyes and mouths, take their hats several feet away and spray them well with bug repellent. Once the caps are donned, the bugs should steer clear.

You need to do your own risk-factor analysis when it comes to using products with DEET. Does eliminating the threat of West Nile or Lyme justify using a product capable of dissolving the frames of your glasses? Maybe.

Clothing with Insect Repellent

If the idea of slathering your babies in toxic bug repellent to protect them from ticks, mosquitoes, and chiggers is, well, repellent to you, consider clothing with insect repellent. Go the do-it-yourself route by using a spray-on bug repellent designed for clothing. These sprays contain bug-defying permethrin, a synthetic substance that mimics the insect repellent found naturally in chrysanthemum plants. During the Napoleonic Wars, French soldiers reportedly used a powder from dried and crushed chrysanthemum flowers to combat fleas and lice. Once a garment is treated, the repellent lasts through six washings. (Sawyer makes spray-on repellents for clothing.)

If you don't want to be bothered with the potentially messy process of spraying existing clothes, you can buy outdoor clothing and gear with built-in permethrin. A company called Insect Shield creates protective clothing by bonding the insect-repelling ingredient directly to the fabric.

The fishing supply company Kids Katch has socks, T-shirts, and bandanas with Insect Shield. Your pooch can even wear the bandana to keep fleas at bay. Outdoor Research makes a wide-brimmed kid's sun hat with built-in bug repellent. Insect Shield can also be found in sleeping bag liners and mesh bug tents from Sea to Summit, and in hammocks from Eagle's Nest Outfitters (ENO). The Travel Chair makes a camp chair with Insect Shield. Of course, if your recliner is your sole line of defense, you may get munched the minute you vacate your seat.

Unlike bug sprays and lotions designed for the skin, garments with Insect Shield or spray-on permethrin are odorless and don't need to be kept out of reach of children.

Treating Bug Bites

Insects are tenacious. Despite your best efforts, you may get chomped while camping with the family. Be prepared to treat kids for bug bites. Once you've been bitten, the body's immune system responds to the insect's saliva by releasing histamine, which causes that maddening itch. Aggressive scratching can release additional histamine, making the itch worse, and can eventually lead to infection.

SMART TIP Cut children's nails short before a camping trip. With a good manicure, kids will collect less dirt and germs under their nails, and they'll do less damage to themselves when scratching bug bites.

If a bite really smarts, put some ice from the cooler into a clean plastic bag, cover the bite with a bandana or paper towel, and apply the ice to reduce inflammation and pain. A cold, clean washcloth can similarly help soothe the itch.

Topical antihistamines, anti-inflammatories, calamine lotion, and hydrocortisone cream can all provide some measure of relief.

Look for products that add natural soothing agents. Aveeno has an over-the-counter 1 percent hydrocortisone cream with oatmeal. Hyland's Bug Bite ointment uses calendula and echinacea. Pain-relieving menthol and camphor combine with soothing essential oils like lavender and lemongrass in Burt's Bees bug bite relief.

Many campers swear by home remedies, such as applying a paste of baking soda and water to a bite. And if you happen to be packing Preparation H hemorrhoid cream (you have my sympathy), you can use it to relieve the itch of a bug bite.

If the itch transcends the usual discomfort, oral antihistamines like Benadryl can help. Of course, if a reaction turns serious (swelling, rash, wheezing, or difficulty breathing), seek medical attention.

Extracting Ticks

When my daughter was two, we found a tick in her scalp. Thankfully she was darn near bald, so the critter was easy to spot. "We need to burn it off!" my husband said in a panic. Before he grabbed for the matches, I suggested we ask Mr. Google how to remove a tick. Sure enough, the first website we found warned, "Don't even think about burning the little bugger off."

 After a camping trip that included tromps through tick-infested woods, wash all your clothes, then tumble them in the dryer for an hour on high heat to kill any stowaways.

There are plenty of folk remedies for removing ticks—like smothering them with nail polish or petroleum jelly—but according to the CDC, the safest, most effective way is to grasp the tick with fine-tipped tweezers and gently pull upward with steady pressure until the tick lets go.

You can find a host of clever tick-removal tools with slots, tweezers, and magnifying glasses (Tick Nipper and Tick Key, to name a few). But tweezers work just fine. Once the tick is out, swab the site with alcohol.

If your child develops a fever, rash, or flu-like symptoms in the next several weeks, or if a red, target-like ring develops at the bite site or elsewhere on the body—a telltale sign of Lyme disease—be suspicious and seek medical attention.

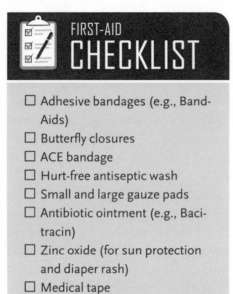

FIRST-AID CHECKLIST

- ☐ Adhesive bandages (e.g., Band-Aids)
- ☐ Butterfly closures
- ☐ ACE bandage
- ☐ Hurt-free antiseptic wash
- ☐ Small and large gauze pads
- ☐ Antibiotic ointment (e.g., Bacitracin)
- ☐ Zinc oxide (for sun protection and diaper rash)
- ☐ Medical tape
- ☐ Moleskin for blisters
- ☐ Fine-pointed tweezers
- ☐ Nail scissors
- ☐ Thermometer
- ☐ Safety pins
- ☐ Ibuprofen (e.g., Motrin or Advil; children's and adult)
- ☐ Acetaminophen (e.g., Tylenol; children's and adult)
- ☐ Antihistamine (e.g., Benadryl; children's and adult)
- ☐ Anti-itch remedy

Soothing Bee Stings

If your child gets a bee sting, it's important to get the stinger out as soon as possible. Scrape it away with a butter knife, a credit card, even a stiff playing card. If you can tell which way the stinger came into the skin, scrape in the opposite direction. Using tweezers or your fingers can push more venom into the skin.

Clean the wound with alcohol or soap and water, dab it with antibiotic ointment, and apply ice. A paste of baking soda and water may help neutralize bee venom. Oral antihistamines can relieve any itching; oral pain relievers (ibuprofen or acetaminophen) can mitigate pain.

If your child is allergic to bees, they may experience symptoms that range from mild (redness, pain, and swelling at the sting site) to severe (hives, difficulty breathing, and swelling of the face, throat, and mouth). If you know your child is allergic to bee stings, surely you have an epinephrine autoinjector

- ☐ Insect repellent
- ☐ 1 percent hydrocortisone cream
- ☐ Sunscreen
- ☐ Hand sanitizer
- ☐ Antacid tablets
- ☐ Cough drops
- ☐ Lubricating eyedrops
- ☐ Instant cold pack
- ☐ Safety whistle
- ☐ Emergency blanket
- ☐ Duct tape

SMART TIP Clip toenails before a hike. Long toenails squished into hiking boots can lead to little blisters or scratched toes.

and know the proper drill: use the EpiPen and call 911.

Always scout out the precise location of the closest emergency room, just in case anyone in your camping party has an allergic reaction to a bee sting—or any urgent medical need, for that matter. This is extra important if the campground is out of cell coverage for an emergency call.

BLISTERS

On hikes, you need to wear good sturdy shoes and synthetic hiking socks. If you've ever gone for a long hike in new boots, you know hiking shoes should be broken in first to avoid blisters. Before you go on a substantial hike, have kids break in new trail shoes by wearing them around town or to school for a few days. Even with well-worn hiking boots, be prepared for blisters by carrying plenty of Band-Aids and moleskin. Carry a small pair of scissors to cut the moleskin to the right size and shape.

As you hike, check in with kids periodically to see if they're developing any hot spots. If they start to feel a rub, don't wait until it's a full-blown, fluid-filled, hike-ending blister. Cut out a donut of moleskin and put it around the hot spot. This will push the offending part of the shoe off the sore spot.

If you didn't pack moleskin or Band-Aids, stop hot spots from becoming blisters by covering them with a piece of duct tape.

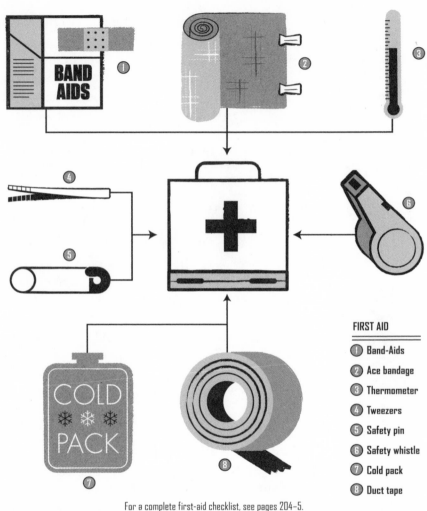

FIRST AID

1 Band-Aids
2 Ace bandage
3 Thermometer
4 Tweezers
5 Safety pin
6 Safety whistle
7 Cold pack
8 Duct tape

For a complete first-aid checklist, see pages 204–5.

FIRST AID

Here's a universal truth: kids get boo-boos, lots and lots of them. Skinned knees and stubbed toes are the stuff of childhood. And when kids are running through the woods over rocks and roots and sticks and slippery leaves, the likelihood of them incurring small injuries increases tenfold. I completely fabricated that statistic. Nevertheless, being armed with a well-stocked first-aid kit is more important once you start camping with the whole ménage.

SMART TIP

In a pinch, you can use a panty liner in place of gauze on a wound. Or use a tampon to stop a bad bloody nose. Cut off the string first, and no one will be the wiser.

A doctor friend of mine told me about a patient who wanted a narcotics prescription for his child, just in case the little nipper broke a leg while backcountry skiing (a totally unethical request, by the way). The couple already had a splint and rescue litter at the ready. My advice: be prepared but not paranoid. Then again, perhaps five-year-olds shouldn't be skiing femur-splintering slopes deep in the backcountry. But maybe that's just me.

You can buy basic, prepackaged first-aid kits at camp stores, or just put your own together. You'll need essentials such as tweezers, ibuprofen, and antibiotic ointment. But for kids, you'll also need child-specific items like a thermometer, Children's Tylenol, and Children's Benadryl. You'll need copious amounts of adhesive bandages. For my kids, a Band-Aid is two parts psychological, one part functional. Even if there's not a drop of blood in sight, a Scooby-Doo Band-Aid has the power to heal.

ACHES, PAINS, PESKY PLANTS, AND BUGS

Chapter Ten

GENERAL SAFETY IN THE GREAT OUTDOORS

George was lost and all alone. He felt tired and stopped to rest. At first he was worried—he was very far from camp. But there were lots of other animals to keep him company. He saw a lizard sunning on a rock and a squirrel chattering in a tree. Then he saw the tail of a black and white kitty peeking out from under a tree. Would the kitty like to play? George gently pulled the kitty out...

—*Curious George Goes Camping* by Margret and H. A. Rey

Ever notice that those fairy tales from the Brothers Grimm never take place at the shopping mall? Hansel and Gretel, Snow White, Little Red Riding Hood—they always end up in the woods.

Evidently, the wilderness is a scary place. You'd be safer sitting in a Barcalounger in the basement, eating s'more-flavored Clif Bars with the AC cranked and the Discovery Channel on the television, than you would be camping outside. Or would you?

Staying at home is not without risk. There's carbon monoxide, slippery bathtubs, mold, medicine cabinets filled with drugs. The potentially fatal brown recluse spider is often found indoors. Say, in the cozy confines of a Barcalounger. A study of national parks in California from 1993 to 1995 showed that in 100,000 visits, only 9.2 injuries or illnesses occurred.[1] Meanwhile, a study of playground equipment by the Consumer Product Safety Committee showed a rate of 75 injuries for every 100,000 people in 1999. Among children aged five to fourteen, there were 348 injuries per 100,000.[2] One might conclude from these statistics that a hike in the woods is safer than swinging from the monkey bars.

But what about lions, tigers, and bears? According to a study in the journal *Wilderness & Environmental Medicine,* the majority of deaths in the United States caused by animal attacks—including bites from snakes, spiders, bees, dogs, and rats, as well as pecks by birds and pokes by porcupine quills—happen *at home.*[3] Which is to say, not while camping. Life, regardless of where you are, is filled with potential pitfalls.

Not to mention, kids do not get hooked on the outdoors by staying indoors. Nor do parents get rejuvenated by rigorous hikes in the fresh air this way. To connect with nature and truly engage with your kids, you need to get on out there. Ultimately the rewards outweigh the risk. Embrace, but be prepared for, the elements of nature: wind, fire, water, earth.

On a float trip through Ruby and Horsethief Canyons on the Colorado River, we took particular care with water safety. Everyone wore PFDs in the rafts, and the kids wore them while wading knee-deep in the river. Adults took turns supervising the children on shore.

Unbeknownst to us, it was the wind we should have been wary of. Just after dinner, a freak windstorm blew in, seemingly out of nowhere. At first, plastic cups and empty baggies started to fly. Then full bowls of pasta and a camp stove—still lit. The kids huddled behind rocks with their eyes shut tightly against the sandblasting force of the wind.

Suddenly I saw one of our party's tents, fully loaded with camp gear, go cartwheeling through the air. It landed in the middle of the river, fully erect, where it instantly floated downstream. My husband asked, all in a dither, "Oh, my God! Whose tent was that?"

In a calm voice and with typical British reserve, my friend Helen responded, "I do believe that was ours." The next day, we found the tent, in

PACK NAVIGATION TOOLS, IN CASE TWO ROADS DIVERGE IN A YELLOW WOOD

NAVIGATION TOOLS

Map

Compass

Mobile phone

GPS

SUMMIT 1.5 MI

SUMMIT .2 MI

SUMMIT 1.3 MI

For a complete backcountry travel essentials checklist, see page 215.

GENERAL SAFETY

shreds, one state to the west. PS: The next morning, Helen's five-year-old daughter said, with identical composure, "Well, I didn't expect to see a bear." Sure enough, across the river, a great big black bear was ambling along the banks.

It was an eventful trip. The takeaway message is this: be prepared and stay calm. Avoid what's known in wilderness-survival circles as "Acute Bad-Judgment Syndrome." Know that you will stay safe most of the time, and when you do meet with adversity in the wild, chances are it will be surmountable. Although our friends lost a great deal of gear (cell phones, wallet, GPS, a favorite stuffed frog), no one was hurt. And in short order, the adventure has become family folklore for all of us. It is a story our kids will tell their kids.

This chapter offers a host of advice on basic safety in the woods, including information on backcountry navigation, animal encounters, sun protection, thunder and lightning, drinking water, and water safety. If you want to dig deeper into the field of wilderness medicine—to go beyond basic first aid and be truly prepared for all medical eventualities—pick up a copy of Buck Tilton's *Backcountry First Aid and Extended Care*, fifth edition.

BACKCOUNTRY NAVIGATION

If you're car camping with kids, you'll likely be doing simple hikes on well-marked trails. Most of the time, other than following an obvious trail and watching for trail blazes, there won't be much navigation involved.

Yet things can go awry even in the seemingly clearest of situations. On one backpacking trip with another family, we consulted a map at the trailhead and made an erroneous assumption about the orientation of the map. With three small kids in tow, we hiked obliviously for half an hour in the opposite direction of our campsite. Eventually, the other dad pulled out a topographic map and compass, and we were able to right ourselves. By then, the directional snafu had added an hour to our hike—a lifetime on the trail to a four-year-old.

So, when you venture into the forest, it's best to be prepared with navigational and contingency tools like map, compass, GPS, and cell phone.

Map and Compass: Old-School Navigation

If you're going on a lengthy hike with kids, especially if the trail system is confusing or requires route finding, you'd be wise to carry a topographic map and compass. Of course, you'll need to know how to use said navigation tools. The websites www.compassdude.com and http://education.usgs .gov are good resources for learning how to use a map and compass. Look for how-to books on compass use and orienteering, or take a navigation class through a local outdoor club or at REI.

GPS: New-School Navigation

If you're a gear wonk with deep pockets, consider a GPS, or Global Positioning System. Borrowing technology originally used by the military, these handheld devices pinpoint your exact location by capturing waves of data beamed down from satellites orbiting the earth. These powerful tools can tell you precisely where you are and help you plot out a path to your destination. Tracking features allow you to keep a record of your route so you can retrace your steps back to the trailhead. The tracking system is not unlike Hansel's trail of bread crumbs, but considerably more effective—unless a bird eats your GPS.

A GPS should never replace old-school navigation tools—the compass and map. By its nature, a GPS can fail you in the field. A dense canopy of trees or deep canyon walls can affect a GPS's reception. Batteries die, motherboards and microchips go kablooey. To learn about using a GPS for fun, see "Geocaching: High-Tech Hide-and-Seek," page 137.

Cell Phones: The Backup Plan

Although you don't want to rely on a cell phone as the keystone of your backwoods emergency plan, carrying a cell phone is a good backup plan in case

GENERAL SAFETY

things go south. The trouble with relying on a cell phone is something called offsetting behavior. People tend to take additional risks when they feel like they have some measure of added protection. Drivers in cars with antilock brakes tend to drive faster and tailgate more, and skiers who wear helmets ski faster than those without.

So, with a cell phone at your disposal, you might hike deeper into the backcountry or leave the first-aid kit behind, thinking you can simply call for help with the touch of a screen. And that may be true. Unless you happen to be out of range or your battery dies. So go ahead, bring the phone. But use your noodle first and go into the woods prepared.

Lost in the Woods: Staying Found

A child lost in the wild is, rightly so, one of a parent's biggest worries. Kids run ahead on hikes or wander off chasing butterflies. But with a little common sense and preparation, it's easy enough to keep your kids found. Kids should stay within talking distance of adults on hiking trails. If you have to yell to be heard, they've strayed too far.

At the campsite, set a perimeter for how far children can explore. The older the child, the wider the perimeter might be. We like to use the same sight rule we employ during hikes: we need to be able to see the kids, and the kids need to be able to see us.

When it comes to toddlers and crawling babies, you have to watch them every minute. When there are camp chores to be done, take shifts watching the children. One parent pounds stakes, and one parent looks after the little ones. When Quinn was around three, I surreptitiously followed him as he wandered away from the campsite, just to see how far he might go if left to his own devices. He toddled about a quarter mile before he even turned around.

Teach kids that if they ever do get lost in the woods, they need to stay put. Tell them to hug a tree: this helps ease panic, reduce injuries from falls, and keeps kids from roaming aimlessly. For more info on the Hug-A-Tree and Survive program for kids, log on to www.nasar.org, the website for the

SMART TIP

The internationally recognized distress signal is three short blasts on a safety whistle.

National Association for Search & Rescue (NASAR). Each child should have, at the very least, a safety whistle on a string around the neck and a large garbage bag to use as an emergency shelter.

To facilitate a search, NASAR recommends taking an imprint of your children's feet before you go into the wilderness. This way trackers can easily identify and follow your child's footprints. Simply set a piece of tinfoil on a folded towel and have the child step on the foil with both feet. Especially if you have more than one child, be sure to label the footprints. According to NASAR, the most important thing parents can do if a child becomes lost is to call for help immediately. The longer you wait, the larger the search area becomes.

Backcountry Travel Essentials
CHECKLIST

- ☐ Food
- ☐ Water
- ☐ First-aid kit
- ☐ Matches and emergency tinder
- ☐ Emergency blanket or large trash bag
- ☐ Map and compass
- ☐ Safety whistle
- ☐ Headlamp or flashlight
- ☐ Extra layers
- ☐ Rain gear
- ☐ Pocketknife
- ☐ Sunglasses and sunscreen

SMALL ANIMAL SAFETY: KEEPING PESKY CRITTERS AT BAY

One of my most memorable childhood camping moments involved a close encounter with a surfeit of skunks. My family and my elementary school BFF were gathered in chairs around the fire on a camping trip to the Delaware Water Gap. As we were roasting our marshmallows, out of the dark woods ambled a pair of skunks and their kits. They waddled in our direction,

GENERAL SAFETY

and we froze, petrified of the imminent danger of *Extremous stinkitus*. They inched closer and closer. We drew up our legs and hugged our knees as the skunks circumnavigated our campfire, literally walking under our feet. I don't think anyone took a breath until the skunks were swallowed up again by the night woods.

The upshot: skunks like marshmallows. Also true is that squirrels like nuts, chipmunks like bread crumbs, little brown birds like strawberry pancakes, and raccoons will eat anything. It's important for your safety to keep your food secure and your campsite free of trash and food scraps. Rodents can carry disease, and even a squirrel can be downright nasty when cornered. For more on keeping critters out of your campsite, see "Camp Kitchen Cleanup," page 111.

BIG ANIMAL SAFETY

Probably the worst thing you can do before a camping trip is read Bill Bryson's *A Walk in the Woods*. It's filled with sensational stories about campers getting mauled by bears and hikers getting stalked and killed by mountain lions. It is fascinating reading, but alarmist. Bears and mountain lions are a danger that is certainly not to be taken lightly, because they sure as heck can kill you. But if you take precautions, and camp and hike smart, your chances of an animal attack are minimal.

In the ten-year period from 1993 through 2002, out of thirty million visitors to Yellowstone National Park, there were fifteen injuries due to bears. All injuries except one occurred in the backcountry. That is to say, only one injury in thirty million visits took place in the developed areas of the park.[4] According to the National Park Service, the chance of being injured by a bear while in Yellowstone is roughly 1 in 1.9 million.[5] You're nearly twice as likely to get struck by lightning. The yearly odds: 1 in 1 million.[6] For additional info on wild animal safety, see "Wildlife Watching," page 132.

Bears

I had my first bear encounter when I was backpacking in the Adirondacks with my sister Cathy and my Irish cousin Deirdre. We had pitched our tent near a lean-to, strung our food bag between two trees, and headed off for a glorious day hike to a high alpine lake.

When we got back, we found a long note from a forest ranger, who very politely listed the mistakes we had made in our short time in the woods. We weren't supposed to pitch our tent so close to a lean-to, for one. And our food bag wasn't strung up high enough. In fact, wrote the ranger, she had seen a bear across the river while writing this very note.

"Crikey! Do you think we'll see a bear?" my cousin asked in an excited brogue.

I looked up to see a big old black bear waddling straight for us. Or more to the point, toward our food bag, which was swinging enticingly low in the breeze. "It's going to be a lot sooner than you think," I said.

"*Shhh*, don't scare it," whispered my sister, who is very smart but has little sense. You'll recall the poison ivy incident.

Now, here is where reading the bulletin board at the ranger station pays off. The warning posters said to scare off bears by making loud noises, like clapping or banging pots together. I started yelling "Go away, bear! Go away!" while clapping like a madwoman. The bear turned heel and tottered off.

While it's possible to scare bears off, it's best to avoid encounters in the first place by hiking in groups and making plenty of noise. Given enough space and time, bears will steer clear of humans. Most dangerous interactions result when a bear is surprised, when you get too close to a mama bear and her cubs, or if you get near a bear and its dinner. Just like people, bears have a personal space bubble—anywhere from fifty to a hundred yards—and you want to stay out of it. Mountain bikers zipping down a curvy single track have been known to literally run into bears. For the record, you do not want to get up close and personal with *Ursus arctos horribilis* (which is the fancy name for a grizzly bear).

Black bears tend to be nonconfrontational. "The chances of being charged by a black bear are zilch, unless you're a biologist working closely with bears or a ninny feeding roadside bears in a national park," says David Smith in *Backcountry Bear Basics: The Definitive Guide to Avoiding Unpleasant Encounters.*[7] When you're in grizzly territory, it's even more important to avoid surprising bears, because grizzlies can be downright surly. When you're rounding a blind curve on a trail, call loudly, "Hey, bear! Coming through!" To further identify yourself as human, you can yodel like a Swiss milkmaid or sing with feeling, maybe something by Cat Stevens.

SMART TIP If you're traveling in bear territory, keep a can of bear spray on a hip holster or chest harness, where you can access it instantly. Bear spray is superhot pepper delivered in a powerful blast from a pressurized can. Clearly you'll need to keep this spray away from the kids.

If you come upon a bear, talk calmly and raise your arms to make yourself look large. Pick up small children and stay close together as a group. You can very slowly back away at an angle, but if the bear approaches, hold your ground. Don't run. This makes you look like a Happy Meal. Even if a bear charges, you want to stand your ground. If a bear is cheeky and comes boldly into your campsite, clap loudly, bang pots if you have them, and yell at the bear. Something along the lines of "Scram, you big hairy bastard!" might work. In the extremely unlikely event that a bear does attack, fall to the ground on top of your child, with your hands on your neck, and play dead. Once a bear no longer perceives you as a threat, it will likely back off.

You may come across recommendations that propose whistling as a tactic for alerting bears to your presence, but Smith contends that this makes you sound like a tasty marmot. We've strung bear bells around our kids' necks, but the light tinkling sound is questionably effective, especially if you're hiking along a rushing brook. The joke goes like this: How can you tell black bear scat from grizzly bear scat? Answer: Black bear scat has huckleberries and seeds. Grizzly bear scat has huckleberries, seeds, and bear bells.

For more on food storage and bears, see "The Tidy Camp Kitchen: Discouraging Moochers," page 113.

Mountain Lions

Most of the above advice for bears goes for mountain lions, too. Avoid them if you can, travel in groups, make a ruckus as you hike. If you encounter a mountain lion, same initial tactics apply. Make yourself big, talk calmly—but this time, say, "Go away, lion!"

The big difference is how to respond to an attack: if a mountain lion attacks, fight like hell. Because mountain lions are predatory, it's more important than ever to keep small children nearby when hiking in lion country.

CAMPFIRE SAFETY

See "The Campfire: Let the Flames Begin!" page 68.

SUN PROTECTION

When you check the weather before a camping adventure, you cross your fingers and toes for blue skies. But weather that's perfect for playing outdoors isn't the best thing for your health. Too much exposure to the sun's ultraviolet (UV) rays can cause painful sunburns and lay the groundwork for skin cancer later in life. Not to mention wrinkles, age spots, and skin that looks like your grandma's leather handbag. Even on overcast days, as much as 80 percent of the sun's UV rays can sneak through the clouds. Look for broad spectrum sunscreens that protect against both UVB and UVA rays.

WEAR SUN HATS: Wear caps with brims that shade the face. Big floppy hats with wide brims are ideal. If your children will only wear baseball caps, insist that the bills face forward and slather the back of their necks with sunscreen. For more on sun hats, see "Hands and Heads" page 50.

SEEK SHADE: Encourage children to play in the shade rather than in direct sunlight, although they will still need sunscreen. You are not immune to the sun's rays while lazing in the dappled shade of a fluttering aspen grove.

COVER UP: Avoid the perils of the scantily clad by wearing lightweight, long-sleeved shirts and pants. The tighter the weave of the fabric, the better the sun protection. Consider clothing with built-in SPF. For more info, see "Sun Protection: Beyond Sunscreen," page 52.

SLATHER ON THE SUNSCREEN: If you do wear shorts and T-shirts—and most of us do in summer—be sure to apply sunscreen liberally to all exposed skin. The American Academy of Dermatology recommends using sunscreens with at least SPF 30. Every time you apply sunscreen, you should use an ounce of lotion. That's about a shot glass full of sunscreen. Reapply every two hours, or after swimming or sweating.

For small children with sensitive skin, head into the woods with a sunscreen that's proven not to irritate their skin. The backwoods is no place to experiment with new body products on kids. The American Academy of Pediatrics advises keeping babies under six months out of the sun rather than using sunscreen. Lips can burn, too, so don't forget to use a lip balm with SPF 30.

PROTECT YOUR PEEPERS: Eye protection is the perfect excuse to make kids look adorable. You can find cute shades just about anywhere, from the grocery store to the gas station. Just make sure the shades you choose have UV protection.

UV AMPLIFIERS: Water, sand, and snow reflect rays of sunshine, increasing your exposure. And the higher the elevation of your campsite, the stronger the sun's rays.

TAKE A SIESTA: When you're camping, it's hard to avoid peak sun times—from 10 A.M. to 4 P.M.—but if you're in a sunny environment, you might be wise to hike or play early in the morning and retreat to a shady campsite in the afternoon. If everyone in your tribe has an afternoon rest, you can head

ZEUS ON THE LOOSE: THUNDERSTORMS ARE SOMETIMES UNAVOIDABLE WHEN CAMPING

(Fig. A)
SEEK SHELTER IN YOUR VEHICLE
WHEN LIGHTNING STRIKES AT CAMP

(Fig. B)
WHEN HIKING, AVOID PEAKS AND KEEP
LOW TO THE GROUND

For a review of thunder and lightning safety, see pages 222–23.

out for a late afternoon or twilight hike, when the sunbeams aren't burning laser hot.

THUNDER AND LIGHTNING

If your camp destination is known more for precipitation than sun—the Pacific Northwest, for instance—severe rain, thunder, and lightning may be an inevitability. But if at all possible, try to avoid thunderstorms altogether. Check the forecast before you go camping. In mountainous regions, hike in the morning to avoid afternoon storms. Plan to be off mountain summits by noon.

Of course, weather happens. "If thunder roars, go indoors" is sound advice, but not terribly practical when you're camping. You could retreat to a visitor center and linger over the exhibits until the thunder stops. Then, to be safe, linger another thirty minutes. If you're at the campsite, the safest bet is to hang out inside the car. Being inside a fully enclosed metal vehicle is safer than being inside a flimsy tent. Contrary to popular belief, it's the metal roof and sides of the car, not the rubber tires, that protect you from lightning.

Now a confession: when it's two in the morning and the kids are sawing wood like lumberjacks and a storm rolls through, we have chosen not to wake them up and schlep them from tent to car. I'd rather endure ten million volts to my cranium than move three kids in the pouring rain in the dead of night, not to mention having to put up with the resulting crabbiness the next day. It's a personal choice, and an unwise one at that, but I'm just being honest here.

If you're two miles down the trail when thunderheads start barreling your way, indoors isn't an option. If you get caught in a thunderstorm, avoid water, high ground (peaks and ridgetops), open fields, and solitary tall trees. The National Lightning Safety Institute recommends the following: "Seek clumps of shrubs or trees of uniform height. Seek ditches, trenches, or the low ground. Seek a low, crouching position with feet together. Place hands on ears to minimize acoustic shock from thunder."[8]

If you hear a clap of thunder when you're swimming and you're not gunning for one of those Darwin Awards (given to folks who remove themselves from the gene pool through sheer stupidity), do not hesitate: *get out of the water*. Lightning gravitates toward the tallest thing around, and if you're on a large expanse of flat water, that tall thing could be your bobbing head. Although pure water is a bad conductor of electricity, the impurities in lakes and pond water do conduct electricity.

STREAM WATER: DRINK SMART

Stream water often looks clean and clear, but it can harbor harmful disease-causing microscopic bugs—protozoa, bacteria, and viruses. Water gets contaminated when fecal matter from humans and animals makes its way into a water source. And the more people hiking around the wilderness, the greater the chance of contamination. A fast-running, high alpine stream is probably safe to drink, but you just never know. If cattle are grazing nearby or pack animals are sharing the trail, you'd do well to be suspicious about the water.

For car campers, drinking water is mostly a nonissue, really, as campsites have either running water or hand pumps with potable water. Set out on hikes with ample bottles of drinking water, and you don't need to worry about micro-nasties like giardia and cryptosporidium, which can cause some mighty gastrointestinal distress.

If you are backcountry camping or if you run out of water on a long hike, you may need to collect water from a stream or lake. Between the common cold, fevers, and the flu, children get sick enough without adding waterborne illness to the mix, so you'll want to treat the water. Probably the simplest and most effective way to purify water is to bring it to a boil and sustain a rolling boil for three minutes.

Boiling makes sense at a backcountry campsite when you're cooking and boiling water anyway. But for hikes, boiling water is a cumbersome process that takes time and fuel, and requires you to carry a backpacking stove. Portable water filters strain out microscopic bugs to make water safe for drinking. Some use a system composed of hoses, filtering membrane, and pump; others employ gravity. Most are lightweight, easy to use, and get the job done relatively quickly, though they can easily set you back $100 to $200. Look for filters from MSR, Katadyn, Platypus, and Sawyer.

SMART TIP It's wise not to let kids chug down river water, but possibly more important is to be vigilant about washing hands when camping. Fecal matter is the source of many pathogens found in water, so proper hygiene at pottying time might be the more salient preventive strategy for avoiding disease.

Treatment tablets and drops of iodine and chlorine dioxide are an inexpensive and simple way to disinfect water. Plink, plunk, and you're done. Although chemical treatments kill most of the offending microbes found in water, iodine is not effective against crypto, and chlorine dioxide takes four hours to kill the protozoan.

New to the water purification scene are SteriPens, which are handheld, portable UV-light water purifiers that use UV rays to zap and deactivate microbes in water. These devices are small, easy to use, and take minutes to sterilize water. Simply put the illuminated wand in clear water, and agitate. (The devices aren't effective in murky water.) SteriPens are a bit spendy (around $90–$150) and they run on battery power, so backup lithium batteries are advisable.

WATER SAFETY: STAYING AFLOAT

A summertime hike near Eldora, Colorado, nearly turned disastrous for us, and water was the culprit. We were standing above a waterfall on a flat, rocky area with foot-wide rivulets running through it. With Anya in the backpack, I stepped easily over one of the fingers of water. Aidan came to join me. Just as he was about to take my hand and cross, he slipped on a rock that didn't even look wet and plunged feetfirst into the fast-moving water. The moment he hit the water, he started to jet downstream. It didn't matter that he was on the swim team. Thankfully I was already reaching for him, so I was close enough to grab his arm instantly and hold him until a friend could pull him from the water. I get the willies just thinking about it.

I've mentioned this elsewhere in this book, but it bears repeating: if you choose to camp near a body of water, you need to watch the younglings every minute. Fast-moving rivers are especially perilous. A moment's distraction is all it takes. In fact, if you're camping near a river with a strong current, consider having kids on shore wear life jackets, also known as personal flotation devices (PFDs). Take turns as Parent on Duty (POD), water safety division. In lakes and ponds, don't rely on inflated water wings, flotation noodles, or PFDs to keep kids from drowning. You should stay within arm's reach of inexperienced swimmers.

When boating, children should always wear PFDs. It's easiest to enforce this rule if it's an absolute. It's even easier to enforce if you model appropriate behavior by wearing a PFD yourself. To make wearing one more enticing, try PFDs from Stearns. They come decorated with animated characters like Spider-Man and Barbie, as well as butterflies and monkeys. Look for models with between-the-leg straps, which keep vests from hiking up to your child's ears in the water. PFDs should fit snugly and have collars to keep kids' heads up in the water. For more on boating with kids, see "Paddling: Floating with Canoes, Kayaks, and Rafts," page 142.

In a perfect world, your kids have been to so many swim lessons or swim team practices that you regularly check them for gills. Learning to swim is the cornerstone of water safety. Good swim classes will also teach kids not to dive in shallow water, to get out of the water if they hear thunder, to float on their backs, and to tread water.

As kids get more comfortable in the water, have them jump into the deep end *without* their goggles until they can do it easily. Goggles can become so integral to the swim experience that if kids were to fall off a dock and plunge into a lake without goggles, they might panic.

In fact, a very similar scenario happened to my son Aidan at the local pool. He had just started on swim team, and he could swim an entire length of freestyle, no problem. One day, he hopped into the deep end sans goggles. He panicked and had to be rescued by a lifeguard. By the way, you would think a child faced with the prospect of drowning would scream, but he never did: he silently splashed and spluttered wide-eyed until the guard grabbed him.

SMART TIP

At the beach, coach small children to face the ocean so that rogue waves don't knock them over from behind.

If spending time at the ocean figures into your camping trip, you need to take into account the dangers of rip currents, undertows, tides, and waves. Ocean waters present additional challenges compared with the placid waters of the local swimming pool. Ideally the beach will have lifeguards.

PS: Don't trust the lifeguards. More than once I have come to the aid of a foundering child right under the nose of a daydreaming guard.

SMART TIP

Take (or retake) an infant-and-child CPR training class. Protocols change with new scientific findings, so if you haven't taken one lately, it's probably time to dust up your training.

Have kids wear slip-on, rubber water shoes when swimming in natural settings. In ponds, lakes, and at rocky beaches, the bottom could be a minefield of sharp rocks, jagged seashells, and prickly sticks. Water shoes can save you from busting out the first-aid kit. For more info, see "Water Shoes," page 56.

Never let kids dive into water unless you know the depth with absolute certainty. Even in seemingly deep water along a shoreline, unseen renegade rocks can lurk just below the surface. If the water's murky and you can't gauge the depth, institute a nonnegotiable no-diving policy.

NOTES

Introduction

1. C. L. Ogden et al., "Prevalence of High Body Mass Index in U.S. Children and Adolescents, 2007–2008," *Journal of the American Medical Association* 303, no. 3 (2010): 242–49.
2. Cynthia Ogden and Margaret Carroll, "Prevalence of Obesity among Children and Adolescents: United States, Trends, 1963–1965 through 2007–2008," National Center for Health Statistics, *Healthy E-Stat* (2010).
3. Richard Louv, *Last Child in the Woods: Saving Our Children from Nature-Deficit Disorder* (Chapel Hill, N.C.: Algonquin Books, 2005), 34.
4. Ibid., 97.

Chapter Two. Gearing Up

1. United States Government Accountability Office, "Bottled Water: FDA Safety and Consumer Protections Are Often Less Stringent Than Comparable EPA Protections for Tap Water," *Report to Congressional Requesters,* June 2009: 23, www.gao.gov/new.items/d09610.pdf
2. www.epa.gov/osw/conserve/materials/organics/food/fd-basic.htm. See also Environmental Protection Agency, *Municipal Solid Waste in the United States: 2009 Facts and Figures* (Washington, D.C.: Environmental Protection Agency, 2010), www.epa.gov/wastes/nonhaz/municipal/pubs/msw2009rpt.pdf.
3. William L. Rathje and Cullen Murphy, *Rubbish! The Archaeology of Garbage* (Tucson: University of Arizona Press, 2001), 112.
4. www.podiatrists.org/enewsroom/pressreleases/pressreleases2007/summerfeet.

Chapter Three. The Campsite

1. M. Ian Gilmour et al., "Air Pollutant-Enhanced Respiratory Disease in Experimental Animals," *Environmental Health Perspectives* 109, no. S4 (2001): 619–22.

Chapter Nine. Aches, Pains, Pesky Plants, and Bugs

1. Mark S. Fradin and John F. Day, "Comparative Efficacy of Insect Repellents against Mosquito Bites," *New England Journal of Medicine* 347, no. 1 (2002): 13–18.
2. Edward A. Ross et al., "Insect Repellant Interactions: Sunscreens Enhance Deet (N,N-Diethyl-M-Toluamide) Absorption," *Drug Metabolism & Disposition* 32, no. 8 (2004): 783–85.
3. Fradin and Day, "Comparative Efficacy," 13–18.

Chapter Ten. General Safety in the Great Outdoors

1. R. Montalvo et al., "Morbidity and Mortality in the Wilderness," *Western Journal of Medicine* 168 (1998): 248–54.
2. Consumer Product Safety Committee, "Special Study: Injuries and Death Associated with Children's Playground Equipment," 2001, www.cpsc.gov/library/playgrnd.pdf.
3. Ricky L. Langley and William E. Morrow, "Deaths Resulting from Animal Attacks in the United States," *Wilderness and Environmental Medicine* 8, no. 1 (1997): 8–16.
4. National Park Service, www.nps.gov/yell/naturescience/injurytable.htm.
5. National Park Service, www.nps.gov/yell/naturescience/injuries.htm.
6. National Weather Service, www.weather.gov/om/lightning/medical.htm.
7. David Smith, *Backcountry Bear Basics: The Definitive Guide to Avoiding Unpleasant Encounters*, 2nd ed. (Seattle, Wash.: Mountaineers Books, 2006), 80.
8. National Lightning Safety Institute, www.lightningsafety.com/nlsi_pls/ploutdoor.htm.

PACKING CHECKLISTS

Following is a compilation of all the checklists that appear throughout this book. Downloadable PDFs of these checklists can be found at the author's blog, www.maddogmom.com, and at www.roostbooks.com/thedownanddirtyguide.

HARDWARE

- ☐ Tent (with poles, stakes, and rainfly)
- ☐ Tarp (ground cloth)
- ☐ Extra plastic tarp
- ☐ Rope
- ☐ Vestibule mat
- ☐ Sleeping bags
- ☐ Sleeping pads
- ☐ Pillows
- ☐ Screen house
- ☐ Play tent
- ☐ Camp chairs
- ☐ Lantern and mantles
- ☐ Flashlights or headlamps
- ☐ Spare batteries
- ☐ Day packs
- ☐ Small mallet (for pounding tent stakes)
- ☐ Ax

LITTLE TYKES GEAR

- ☐ Front-loading baby carrier
- ☐ Baby backpack carrier
- ☐ Portable crib
- ☐ Kid-sized day pack
- ☐ Child's reusable water bottle
- ☐ Portable potty or potty seat
- ☐ Portable high chair
- ☐ Child-sized folding camp chair
- ☐ Battery-powered night-light
- ☐ Child-sized or small adult sleeping pad
- ☐ Child-sized sleeping bag

CAMP KITCHEN

- Camp kitchen
- Camp stove
- Fuel
- Pots
- Pans
- Skillet
- Grill rack
- Cutting board
- Sharp knife
- Measuring cup
- Measuring spoons
- Spatula
- Big spoon
- Long-handled tongs
- Strainer
- Plates
- Bowls
- Cups
- Insulated coffee cups

- Water bottles
- Utensils
- Marshmallow sticks
- Corkscrew
- Bottle opener
- Pot lifter
- Aluminum foil
- Small plastic bags
- Large plastic bags
- Plastic tablecloth
- Extra-large tablecloth clips or tablecloth weights
- Tupperware containers
- Matches, lighter, or fire stick
- Collapsible water container
- Water purifier (optional)
- Drink coozies
- Coolers

SOFTWEAR

- Underwear
- Socks
- Base layer, top and bottom
- Fleece shirt
- Fleece pants
- Down jacket
- Zip-off travel pants

- Fleece or down vest
- Fleece hat
- Light gloves
- Rain or shell jacket
- Rain pants
- Shorts

- □ T-shirts
- □ Bathing suit
- □ Sun hat
- □ SPF clothing
- □ Pajamas
- □ Laundry bag

FOOTWEAR

- □ Hiking boots or light hikers
- □ Sneakers
- □ Sandals with straps
- □ Flip-flops
- □ Water shoes
- □ Camp booties

CAMPFIRE

- □ Homemade or store-bought fire-starting tinder
- □ Tinder collected at the campsite
- □ Kindling
- □ Larger sticks
- □ Bundle of firewood
- □ Matches, lighter, or fire starter
- □ Paper or plastic plate

CAMP KITCHEN CLEANUP

- □ Plastic washbasins
- □ Sponge with scouring pad
- □ Small scrubber brush
- □ Old washcloths or tea towels
- □ Biodegradable camp soap (e.g., Dr. Bronner's)
- □ Grocery-store plastic bags (for small amounts of garbage)
- □ Tall kitchen garbage bags
- □ Paper towels
- □ Baby wipes
- □ Clothesline and clothespins

STARGAZING

- □ Binoculars
- □ Small telescope
- □ Star chart
- □ Flashlight covered in red cellophane

- [ ] Mobile phone with stargazing app
- [ ] Reclining camp chair, sleeping pad, or blanket

WILDLIFE WATCHING

- [ ] Child-sized binoculars
- [ ] Field guides
- [ ] Camera with zoom lens
- [ ] Bug collection boxes
- [ ] Magnifying glass
- [ ] Butterfly net
- [ ] Nature journal
- [ ] Pen and pencil

WATER-BASED ACTIVITIES

- [ ] Fishing rods and tackle
- [ ] Bathing suits
- [ ] Goggles
- [ ] Water shoes
- [ ] Towels
- [ ] Personal flotation devices (PFDs)
- [ ] Water wings
- [ ] Dingy

CAMPSITE PLAY

- [ ] Frisbee
- [ ] Soccer ball
- [ ] Hacky Sack
- [ ] Soft football (like a Nerf)
- [ ] Baseball and mitts
- [ ] Lacrosse sticks and ball
- [ ] Little trucks with big tires
- [ ] Bubbles
- [ ] Sand toys
- [ ] Small dolls and action figures
- [ ] Favorite stuffed animal

QUIET TIME

- [ ] Playing cards
- [ ] Kid travel games
- [ ] Travel-sized board games
- [ ] Rope for knot tying

- Camping-themed books
- Flashlight for reading in the tent
- Coloring books or sheets, markers, and crayons

- Clipboard for leaning on while coloring
- Guitar
- Songbook
- Book of spooky stories

BASIC CAMP ART

- Inexpensive digital camera
- Pencils and sharpener
- Sketch pad, coloring sheets, loose paper
- Crayons and markers

- Watercolors and brushes
- Nature journal
- Glue, paper, scissors
- Chalk (for rubbings)

DAILY HYGIENE

- Antimicrobial hand sanitizer
- Baby wipes
- Moisturizing lotion
- Small tube of Aquaphor
- Travel-size deodorant
- Lip balm
- Toothpaste
- Toothbrush
- Dental floss

- Hairbrush
- Soap and shampoo
- Sanitary products
- Washcloth and towel
- Plastic washbasin
- Earplugs
- Needle and thread
- Contacts and glasses
- Prescription medication

BACKWOODS POTTYING

- Small poop shovel or garden trowel

- Toilet paper or baby wipes in a plastic bag

Diaper rash cream
for babies

- Plastic bag for trash
- Hand sanitizer

FIRST AID

- Adhesive bandages (e.g., Band-Aids)
- Butterfly closures
- ACE bandage
- Hurt-free antiseptic wash
- Small and large gauze pads
- Antibiotic ointment (e.g., Bacitracin)
- Zinc oxide (for sun protection and diaper rash)
- Thermometer
- Ibuprofen (e.g., Motrin or Advil; children's and adult)
- Acetaminophen (e.g., Tylenol; children's and adult)
- Antihistamine (e.g., Benadryl; children's and adult)
- Nail scissors

- Medical tape
- Safety pins
- Insect repellent
- Anti-itch remedy
- 1 percent hydrocortisone cream
- Sunscreen
- Hand sanitizer
- Antacid tablets
- Cough drops
- Lubricating eyedrops
- Instant cold pack
- Safety whistle
- Emergency blanket
- Duct tape
- Moleskin for blisters
- Fine-pointed tweezers

BACKCOUNTRY TRAVEL ESSENTIALS

- Food
- Water
- First-aid kit
- Matches and emergency tinder

- Emergency blanket or large trash bag
- Map and compass
- Safety whistle

- ☐ Headlamp or flashlight
- ☐ Extra layers
- ☐ Rain gear
- ☐ Pocketknife
- ☐ Sunglasses and sunscreen

RESOURCES

BOOKS

Informational and How-To Books

Bell, Annie. *The Camping Cookbook*. London: Kyle Books, 2011.

Brandt, DeAnna. *Nature Log Kids: A Kid's Journal to Record Their Nature Experiences*. Cambridge, Minn.: Adventure Publications, 1998.

Brunelle, Lynn. *Camp Out! The Ultimate Kids' Guide*. New York: Workman Publishing, 2007.

Buchanan, Eugene. *Outdoor Parents, Outdoor Kids: A Guide to Getting Your Kids Active in the Great Outdoors*. Beachburg, Ont.: Heliconia Press, 2010.

Carlson, Laurie. *Kids Camp! Activities for the Backyard or Wilderness*. Chicago: Chicago Review Press, 1995.

Driscoll, Michael. *A Child's Introduction to the Night Sky: The Story of the Stars, Planets, and Constellations—and How You Can Find Them in the Sky*. New York: Black Dog & Leventhal, 2004.

Kane, Tracy. *Fairy Houses*. Lee, N.H.: Light-Beams, 2001.

Leslie, Clare Walker, and Charles E. Roth. *Keeping a Nature Journal: Discover a Whole New Way of Seeing the World around You*. North Adams, Mass.: Storey, 2003.

Meyer, Kathleen. *How to Shit in the Woods: An Environmentally Sound Approach to a Lost Art*. New York: Ten Speed Press, 1989.

Monaghan, Kimberly. *Organic Crafts: 75 Earth-Friendly Art Activities*. Chicago: Chicago Review Press, 2007.

Olmstead, Adrienne. *My Nature Journal: A Personal Nature Guide for Young People*. Lafayette, Calif.: Pajaro, 2000.

Penn, Randy. *The Handy Box of Knots: Useful Knots for Every Situation, Indoors and Out.* New York: Sterling Innovation, 2008.

Sohi, Morteza E. *Look What I Did with a Leaf.* New York: Walker, 1993.

Tilton, Buck. *Backcountry First Aid and Extended Care,* 5th edition. Guilford, Conn.: Falcon Press Publishing, 2007.

Walke, Ted and Linda. *Boating Safety "Sidekicks" Go Fishing.* Harrisburg, Pa.: Within Reach, 2002.

Wallace, Mary. *Make Your Own Inuksuk.* Toronto: Maple Tree Press, 2004.

Inspirational Books

Brett, Jan. *Hedgie Blasts Off!* New York: Putnam Juvenile, 2006.

Ehlert, Lois. *Leaf Man.* New York: Harcourt, 2005.

Forgey, William. *Campfire Tales: Ghoulies, Ghosties, and Long-Leggety Beasties.* Guilford, Conn.: Globe Pequot Press, 1999.

Goldsworthy, Andy. *Hand to Earth: Andy Goldsworthy Sculpture 1976–1990.* New York: Harry N. Abrams, 1990.

———. *Passage.* New York: Harry N. Abrams, 2004.

Lewis, Meriwether, and William Clark. *The Journals of Lewis and Clark.* Edited by Frank Bergon. New York: Signet Classic, 2002.

Stine, R. L. *Beware! R. L. Stine Picks His Favorite Scary Stories.* New York: Parachute, 2002.

Nature- and Camping-Themed Picture Books

Berenstain, Stan and Jan. *The Berenstain Bears Blaze a Trail.* New York: Random House, 1985.

Berry, Lynne. *Duck Tents.* New York: Henry Holt, 2009.

Brett, Jan. *The Mitten.* New York: Putnam Juvenile, 1989.

———. *The Umbrella.* New York: Putnam, 2004.

Brown, M. K. *Let's Go Camping with Mr. Sillypants.* New York: Crown, 1995.

Christelow, Eileen. *Jerome Camps Out.* New York: Clarion Books, 1998.

Creech, Sharon. *Fishing in the Air.* New York: Joanna Cotler Books, 2000.

DiPucchio, Kelly. *Sipping Spiders through a Straw: Campfire Songs for Monsters*. New York: Scholastic Press, 2008.

George, William T. *Box Turtle at Long Pond*. New York: Greenwillow Books, 1989.

Holabird, Katharine. *Angelina and Henry*. Middleton, Wis.: Pleasant Company Publications, 2002.

Hundal, Nancy. *Camping*. Markham, Ont.: Fitzhenry and Whiteside, 2006.

Hunger, Anne. *Possum and the Peeper*. New York: Houghton Mifflin, 2000.

Isaacs, Anne. *Pancakes for Supper*. New York: Scholastic Press, 2006.

James, Helen Foster. *S Is for S'mores: A Camping Alphabet*. Ann Arbor, Mich.: Sleeping Bear Press, 2007.

Kent, Jack. *The Caterpillar and the Polliwog*. New York: Aladdin, 1985.

Kvasnosky, Laura McGee. *Frank & Izzy Set Sail*. Cambridge, Mass.: Candlewick Press, 2004.

Lakin, Patricia. *Camping Day!* New York: Dial Books, 2009.

Orr, Wendy. *The Princess and Her Panther*. New York: Beach Lane Books, 2010.

Polacco, Patricia. *The Graves Family Goes Camping*. New York: Philomel Books, 2005.

Rey, Margret and H. A. *Curious George Goes Camping*. New York: Houghton Mifflin, 1999.

———. *Curious George Goes Hiking*. New York: Houghton Mifflin, 1985.

Ross, Tony. *I Want to Do It Myself: A Little Princess Story*. London: Andersen Press, 2010.

Say, Allen. *The Lost Lake*. New York: Houghton Mifflin, 1989.

Shaw, Nancy. *Sheep Take a Hike*. New York: Houghton Mifflin, 1994.

Singer, Marilyn. *In My Tent*. New York: Macmillan, 1992.

———. *Quiet Night*. New York: Clarion Books, 2002.

Stern, Maggie. *Acorn Magic*. New York: Greenwillow Books, 1998.

Wargin, Kathy-jo. *Scare a Bear*. Ann Arbor, Mich.: Sleeping Bear Press, 2010.

Wolff, Ashley. *Stella and Roy Go Camping*. New York: Dutton Children's Books, 1999.

Wolff, Ferida. *Watch Out for Bears! The Adventures of Henry and Bruno*. New York: Random House, 1999.

Camping-Themed Easy Readers

Eastman, Peter. *Fred and Ted Go Camping*. New York: Beginner Books, 2005.

Hanson, Dave. *We're Going Camping: Now What?* London: Franklin Watts Books, 2004.

Harvey, Alex. *Olivia Goes Camping*. New York: Simon Spotlight, 2011.

Herman, Gail. *The Camping Caper: Scooby-Doo Readers No. 18*. New York: Scholastic, 2006.

Katschke, Judy. *Take a Hike, Snoopy!* New York: Little Simon, 2002.

Koontz, Robin Michal. *Chicago and the Cat: The Camping Trip*. New York: Cobblehill Books, 1994.

Manushkin, Fran. *Katie Goes Camping*. Mankato, Minn.: Picture Window Books, 2010.

Meister, Cari. *Tiny Goes Camping*. New York: Viking, 2006.

Parish, Peggy. *Amelia Bedelia Goes Camping*. New York: Greenwillow Books, 1985.

Rylant, Cynthia. *Henry and Mudge and the Starry Night*. New York: Simon & Schuster, 1998.

Sadler, Marilyn. *P. J. Funnybunny Camps Out*. New York: Random House, 1993.

Spohn, Kate. *Turtle and Snake Go Camping*. New York: Penguin Putnam, 2000.

Suen, Anastasia. *The Scary Night: A Robot and Rico Story*. Mankato, Minn.: Stone Arch Books, 2010.

Yolen, Jane. *The Giants Go Camping*. New York: Seabury Press, 1979.

Camping-Themed Chapter Books for Young Readers

Brooks, Walter R. *Freddy Goes Camping*. New York: Puffin Books, 2003.

Conford, Ellen. *Annabel the Actress: Starring in Camping It Up*. New York: Simon & Schuster, 2004.

Dixon, Franklin W. *Danger on Vampire Trail: The Hardy Boys, No. 50*. New York: Grosset & Dunlap, 1971.

Hermes, Patricia. *Emma Dilemma and the Camping Nanny*. Tarrytown, N.Y.: Marshall Cavendish Children, 2009.

Holt, Kimberly Willis. *Piper Reed: Campfire Girl*. New York: Henry Holt, 2010.

Kerrin, Jessica Scott. *Martin Bridge: Blazing Ahead!* Toronto: Kids Can Press, 2006.

Kimpton, Diana. *Pony-Crazed Princess: Princess Ellie's Camping Trip*. New York: Hyperion Paperbacks for Children, 2006.

Klein, Abby. *Ready, Freddy! Camping Catastrophe*. New York: Blue Sky Press, 2008.

L'Engle, Madeleine. *The Moon by Night: The Austin Family Chronicles, Book 2*. New York: Square Fish, 2008.

Look, Lenore. *Alvin Ho: Allergic to Camping, Hiking, and Other Natural Disasters*. New York: Schwartz & Wade Books, 2009.

Meadows, Daisy. *Cara the Camp Fairy*. New York: Scholastic, 2011.

Pearson, Susan. *The Campfire Ghosts*. New York: Simon & Schuster Books for Young Readers, 1990.

Pryor, Bonnie. *Vinegar Pancakes and Vanishing Cream*. New York: HarperCollins, 1996.

Salisbury, Graham. *Night of the Howling Dogs*. New York: Wendy Lamb Books, 2007.

Scrimger, Richard. *Noses Are Red*. Toronto: Tundra Books, 2002.

Sedita, Francesco. *Miss Popularity Goes Camping*. New York: Scholastic, 2009.

Warner, Gertrude Chandler. *The Camp-Out Mystery: The Box Car Children, No. 27*. Park Ridge, Ill.: Albert Whitman, 1992.

———. *The Canoe Trip Mystery: The Box Car Children, No. 40.* Park Ridge, Ill.: Albert Whitman, 1994.

Van Draanen, Wendelin. *Sammy Keyes and the Wild Things.* New York: Alfred A. Knopf, 2007.

CAMPING WEBSITES

Organizations

American Hiking Society: www.americanhiking.org

American Park Network: www.ohranger.com

Boy Scouts of America: www.scouting.org

Centers for Disease Control and Prevention: www.cdc.gov

Children & Nature Network: www.childrenandnature.org

Choose Outdoors: www.chooseoutdoors.org

Girl Scouts of the USA: www.girlscouts.org

Leave No Trace: www.lnt.org

National Association of Search and Rescue (Hug-a-Tree and Survive Program): www.nasar.org

National Audubon Society: www.audubon.org

National Park Service: www.nps.gov

National Wildlife Federation (NWF): www.nwf.org/kids

NWF's Great American Backyard Campout: www.backyardcampout.com

The North Face: www.planetexplore.com

Parks Canada: www.pc.gc.ca

Tread Lightly!: www.treadlightly.org

US Geological Survey Education: http://education.usgs.gov

Magazines and Online Camp Resources

Audubon magazine: www.audubonmagazine.org

Backpacker magazine: www.backpacker.com

birdJam: www.birdjam.com

RESOURCES

The Children's Butterfly Site: www.kidsbutterfly.org
Compass Dude: www.compassdude.com
Geocaching: www.geocaching.com
GORP (Great Outdoor Recreation Pages): www.gorp.com
Helen Olsson: www.helen-olsson.com
LowerGear Outdoor Rentals and Sales: www.lowergear.com
Mad Dog Mom (Helen Olsson's blog): www.maddogmom.com
National Audubon Society Family Time: http://education.audubon.org
    /family-time
National Audubon Society Just for Kids: www.audubon.org/educate/kids
National Geographic Kids: www.kids.nationalgeographic.com/kids
Outdoors Geek (online rentals): www.outdoorsgeek.com
Outside magazine: www.outsideonline.com
ReserveAmerica (campsite reservations): www.reserveamerica.com
Woodall's Campground Directory: www.woodalls.com
Woodall's Camping Life magazine: www.campinglife.com

Camping Stores and Catalogues

Byer of Maine: www.byerofmaine.com
Cabela's: www.cabelas.com
Campmor: www.campmor.com
Coghlan's: www.coghlans.com
Eastern Mountain Sports: www.ems.com
L.L.Bean: www.llbean.com
Orvis: www.orvis.com
REI: www.rei.com
Sierra Trading Post: www.sierratradingpost.com

Tents, Sleeping Bags and Pads, Mats, Camp Chairs

Big Agnes: www.bigagnes.com
CGear Sand-Free Technology: www.cgear-sandfree.com

Crazy Creek: www.crazycreek.com
Kelty: www.kelty.com
Marmot: www.marmot.com
Mountain Hardwear: www.mountainhardwear.com
The North Face: www.thenorthface.com
REI: www.rei.com
Sierra Designs: www.sierradesigns.com
Therm-a-Rest: www.cascadedesigns.com
    /therm-a-rest

Car Roof-Top Storage Boxes

Thule: www.thule.com
Yakima: www.yakima.com

Backpacks and Child Carriers

BabyBjörn: www.babybjorn.com
CamelBak: www.camelbak.com
Deuter: www.deuterusa.com
ERGObaby: www.ergobabycarrier.com
GoLite: www.golite.com
Gregory: www.gregorypacks.com
Helly Hansen: www.hellyhansen.com
Kelty: www.kelty.com
Lafuma: www.lafuma.com
Marmot: www.marmot.com
Moby: www.mobywrap.com
Mountain Hardwear: www.mountainhardwear.com
Mountainsmith: www.mountainsmith.com
The North Face: www.thenorthface.com
Osprey: www.ospreypacks.com
Sherpani: www.sherpanichildcarriers.com

Sierra Designs: www.sierradesigns.com
Snugli: www.snugli.com

Headlamps, Flashlights, Lanterns

Black Diamond: www.blackdiamondequipment.com
Brunton: www.bruntonoutdoor.com
Coleman: www.coleman.com
Mammut: www.mammut.ch
Petzl: www.petzl.com
Play Visions: www.playvisions.com
Princeton Tec: www.princetontec.com

Camp Cookware

Camp Chef: www.campchef.com
Coleman: www.coleman.com
GSI Outdoors: www.gsioutdoors.com
Jetboil: www.jetboil.com
Lodge Cast Iron: www.lodgemfg.com
MSR: www.msrcorp.com
Open Country: www.opencountrycampware.com
Primus: www.primuscamping.com
REI: www.rei.com
Rome: www.romeindustries.com
Sea to Summit: www.seatosummit.com
Snow Peak: www.snowpeak.com

Clothing

Arc'teryx: www.arcteryx.com
Columbia: www.columbia.com
ExOfficio: www.exofficio.com
GoLite: www.golite.com

Helly Hansen: www.hellyhansen.com
Icebreaker: www.icebreaker.com
Marmot: www.marmot.com
Molehill Mountain Equipment: www.molehillmtn.com
Mountain Hardwear: www.mountainhardwear.com
The North Face: www.thenorthface.com
Outdoor Research: www.outdoorresearch.com
Patagonia: www.patagonia.com
REI: www.rei.com
Royal Robbins: www.royalrobbins.com
Sierra Designs: www.sierradesigns.com
SmartWool: www.smartwool.com
Solumbra: www.sunprecautions.com

Sun Hats

Columbia: www.columbia.com
Flap Happy: www.flaphappy.com
Outdoor Research: www.outdoorresearch.com
REI: www.rei.com
Sunday Afternoons: www.sundayafternoons.com

Footwear

Chaco: www.chacos.com
Hi-Tec: www.hi-tec.com
Keen: www.keenfootwear.com
Merrell: www.merrell.com
Montrail: www.montrail.com
The North Face: www.thenorthface.com
Speedo: www.speedousa.com
Tecnica: www.tecnicausa.com
Teva: www.teva.com

Tuga: www.tugasunwear.com
Vasque: www.vasque.com

Socks

Bridgedale: www.bridgedale.com
Lorpen: www.lorpen.com
SmartWool: www.smartwool.com
Thorlos: www.thorlo.com
Wigwam: www.wigwam.com

Hydration

CamelBak: www.camelbak.com
Klean Kanteen: www.kleankanteen.com
Nalgene: www.nalgene.com
Platypus: www.cascadedesigns.com/platypus
SIGG: www.sigg.com

Water Purification

Katadyn: www.katadyn.com
MSR: www.msrcorp.com
Platypus: www.cascadedesigns.com/platypus
Potable Aqua: www.potableaqua.com
Sawyer: www.sawyer.com
SteriPen: www.steripen.com

Insect Repellent and Bug Bite Remedies

Adventure Medical Kits: www.adventuremedicalkits.com
BiteBlocker: www.homs.com
Hyland's (Bug Bite Ointment): www.hylands.com
Repel: www.repel.com
Sawyer (Spray-on repellent for clothing): www.sawyer.com

Products with Insect Shield

ENO (Eagles Nest Outfitters): www.eaglesnestoutfittersinc
.com
ExOfficio: www.exofficio.com
Insect Shield: www.insectshield.com
Kid's Katch: www.kidskatch.com
Outdoor Research: www.outdoorresearch.com
Sea to Summit: www.seatosummit.com
TravelChair: www.travelchair.com

Lightning Safety

National Lightning Safety Institute: www.lightningsafety.com
National Weather Service Lightning Safety: www.lightningsafety.noaa
.gov
Struck By Lightning: www.struckbylightning.org

Campfire

Coghlan's: www.coghlans.com
Light My Fire: www.lightmyfireusa.com
Lightning Nuggets: www.lightningnuggets.com
River Connection (Fire pans): www.riverconnection.com
Ultimate Survival Technologies: www.ultimatesurvivaltech.com

Wildlife Watching

National Audubon Society Field Guides: http://marketplace.audubon.org/
products/Audubon%20Books
National Audubon Society Mobile Field Guides and Online Guides: www.
audubonguides.com
National Wildlife Federation Field Guides: www.sterlingpublishing.com
Peterson Field Guides: www.houghtonmifflinbooks.com/peterson

Binoculars

Eagle Optics: www.eagleoptics.com

Fishing and Paddling

Stearns: www.stearnsflotation.com
Team Tacklebox: www.teamtacklebox.com

Stargazing

Kids Astronomy: www.kidsastronomy.com
Nebraska Star Party: www.nebraskastarparty.org
Satellite Flybys: www.spaceweather.com/flybys
Sky & Telescope magazine: www.skyandtelescope.com

Knot Tying

Animated Knots: www.animatedknots.com
Net Knots: www.netknots.com

Singing

KIDiddles: www.kididdles.com
National Institute of Environmental Health Sciences Kids' Pages: http://kids.nieh.nih.gov
Ultimate Camp Resource: www.ultimatecampresource.com

Camp Art

Fairy Houses: www.fairyhouses.com
Flower Pressing: www.thepressedflowerstore.com
Nature Journaling: www.pajaro.com
Playful Learning: www.playfulearning.com

Photo Books and Digital Scrapbooking

CropMom: www.cropmom.com
Jessica Sprague: www.jessicasprague.com
Kodak Gallery: www.kodakgallery.com
Peppermint Creative: www.peppermintcreative.com
Shabby Princess: www.shabbyprincess.com
Shutterfly: www.shutterfly.com
Smilebox: www.smilebox.com
Snapfish: www.snapfish.com
Viovio: www.viovio.com

INDEX

ABOUT THE AUTHOR

Helen Olsson is a freelance writer based in Boulder, Colorado. She is a former executive editor at *Skiing* magazine, where she worked (and skied with great regularity) for ten years. Winner of the Canadian Tourism's Northern Lights Journalism Award for magazine writing and a finalist in the Women's Sports Foundation Sports Journalism Awards, Olsson has written for *Self, Ski, Women's Adventure, Delicious Living, Sports Illustrated for Women,* and *Women's Sports & Fitness.* Her articles about camping with kids have appeared in the *New York Times,* including a story about a llama-trekking trip that was featured in the travel section in August 2009. That adventure was the inspiration for this book.

Olsson first camped with her family as a toddler in the late sixties in the wilds of upstate New York. Subsequent family camping trips in the East and one particularly rainy camp outing with the Girl Scouts left a lasting impact. She now camps often in Colorado and elsewhere in the West with her husband, Jeff, and their three children, Quinn, Aidan, and Anya.